These primers on Jonathan Edwards's passion for God—provide an excellent unto God. And they help the rest of us majesty of our Savior. We owe a great Douglas Sweeney for making Edwards accessible to the rest of us thirsty pilgrims.

D0384034

—**Thabiti Anyabwile**, Pastor of First Baptist Church of Grand Cayman, Cayman Islands

Everyone says Jonathan Edwards is important. Quite frankly, however, his writing style is pretty dense by contemporary standards, so few pastors and other Christian leaders have invested much time reading him. This new series tackles the problem. Here is the kernel of much of Edwards's thought in eminently accessible form.

—**D. A. Carson**, Research Professor of New Testament, Trinity Evangelical Divinity School

In *The Essential Edwards Collection*, Owen Strachan and Doug Sweeney point with knowledge and excitement to clear and searching sections that illuminate God's truth and search our hearts. In this collection, Edwards is introduced to a new generation of readers. His concerns are made our concerns. This is a worthy effort and I pray that God will bless it.

—**Mark Dever**, Senior Pastor, Capitol Hill Baptist Church, Washington, DC

I am deeply impressed with the vision that has brought together this splendid library of volumes to introduce Jonathan Edwards to a new generation. Owen Strachan and Douglas Sweeney have provided an incredible service by making the often challenging writings of America's greatest theologian accessible for seasoned theologians, pastors, and students alike with their five-volume *Essential Edwards Collection*. This series is properly titled the "essential collection."

—**David S. Dockery**, President, Union University

This series is a fantastic introduction to the heart, mind, and ministry of the greatest theologian America has ever produced.
      —**Mark Driscoll**, Pastor of Mars Hill Church, President of the Acts 29 Church Planting Network

Jonathan Edwards was a preacher of the Word, a pastor of souls, a philosopher of first rank, and the greatest theologian America has ever produced. In this wonderful new anthology of Edwards's writings, the great Puritan saint lives again. I can think of no better tonic for our transcendence-starved age than the writings of Edwards. But beware: reading this stuff can change your life forever!
      —**Timothy George**, Founding Dean of Beeson Divinity School of Samford University

Let Strachan and Sweeney serve as your guides through the voluminous writings of America's greatest theologian. They have been shaped by his godly counsel and moved by his passion for Christ. By God's grace, Edwards can do the same for you. Start your journey with *The Essential Edwards Collection*.
      —**Collin Hansen**, Author of *Young, Restless, Reformed*

Owen Strachan and Douglas Sweeney have done us all a great service by remixing and reloading the teaching of Jonathan Edwards for a new generation. They do more than introduce us to his writing: they show us how his biblical teaching relates to a modern world and leave us hungry for more. I am very impressed and very grateful for *The Essential Edwards Collection*.
      —**Joshua Harris**, Senior Pastor of Covenant Life Church

From a course he taught at Yale and in personal friendship, Doug Sweeney has taught me much about Edwards. Possessing a command of the academic field, he and Owen Strachan nevertheless write this collection with pastoral concern, showing the relevance of Edwards for our Christian faith and practice today. It's a rare combination of gifts and insights that Sweeney and Strachan bring to this task.

—**Michael Horton**, J. Gresham Machen Professor of Systematic Theology and Apologetics, Westminster Theological Seminary California

When it comes to Jonathan Edwards's writing, where does an average reader (like me!) begin? Right here, with *The Essential Edwards Collection*. Strachan and Sweeney provide a doorway into the life and teaching of one of the church's wisest theologians. The authors have also included notes of personal application to help us apply the life and teaching of Edwards to our own lives. I've read no better introduction to Jonathan Edwards.

—**C. J. Mahaney**, President of Sovereign Grace Ministries

Why hasn't this been done before? *The Essential Edwards Collection* is now essential reading for the serious-minded Christian. Doug Sweeney and Owen Strachan have written five excellent and accessible introductions to America's towering theological genius—Jonathan Edwards. They combine serious scholarship with the ability to make Edwards and his theology come alive for a new generation. *The Essential Edwards Collection* is a great achievement and a tremendous resource. I can't think of a better way to gain a foundational knowledge of Edwards and his lasting significance.

—**R. Albert Mohler Jr.**, President of The Southern Baptist Theological Seminary

A great resource! Edwards continues to speak, and this series of books is an excellent means to hear Jonathan Edwards again live and clear. Pure gold; be wise and invest in it!

—**Dr. Josh Moody**, Senior Pastor, College Church in Wheaton.

You hold in your hands a unique resource: a window into the life and thought of Jonathan Edwards, a man whose life was captured by God for the gospel of Jesus Christ. In these pages you'll not only learn about Edwards, but you'll be able to hear him speak in his own words. This winsome and accessible introduction is now the first thing I'd recommend for those who want to know more about America's greatest pastor-theologian.

—**Justin Taylor**, Managing Editor, ESV Study Bible

Jonathan Edwards is surely one of the most influential theologians of the eighteenth century. Now, at last, we have a wide-ranging and representative sample of his work published in an attractive, accessible and, most important of all, readable form. The authors are to be commended for the work they have put into this set and I hope it will become an important feature of the library of many pastors and students of the Christian faith.

—**Carl R. Trueman**, Academic Dean, Westminster Theological Seminary

JONATHAN EDWARDS
on HEAVEN & HELL

THE ESSENTIAL
EDWARDS
COLLECTION

OWEN STRACHAN *and* DOUGLAS SWEENEY

MOODY PUBLISHERS
CHICAGO

Editor: Christopher Reese
Interior Design: Ragont Design
Cover Design: Gearbox

Library of Congress Cataloging-in-Publication Data

Strachan, Owen.
  Jonathan Edwards on heaven and hell / Owen Strachan and Douglas Sweeney.
    p. cm. — (The essential Edwards collection)
  Includes bibliographical references.
  ISBN 978-0-8024-2461-7
  1. Edwards, Jonathan, 1703-1758. 2. Future life—Christianity. I. Sweeney,
Douglas A. II. Title.
BT903.S77 2010
236'.2—dc22
                                                               2009040816

We hope you enjoy this book from Moody Publishers. Our goal is to provide high-
quality, thought-provoking books and products that connect truth to your real needs
and challenges. For more information on other books and products written and produced from a biblical perspective, go to www.moodypublishers.com or write to:

Moody Publishers
820 N. LaSalle Boulevard
Chicago, IL 60610

1 3 5 7 9 10 8 6 4 2

Printed in the United States of America

The Essential Edwards Collection

Jonathan Edwards: Lover of God

Jonathan Edwards on Beauty

Jonathan Edwards on Heaven and Hell

Jonathan Edwards on the Good Life

Jonathan Edwards on True Christianity

OS

In memory of Daniel Dustin,
who lived with heaven on
his mind and now walks with God

DS

In memory of the Revs. Paul Sweeney and Marvin Turner,
who labored in light of eternity

CONTENTS

Abbreviations of
Works Cited

The following shortened forms of books by or about Jonathan Edwards are used in the text to indicate the source of quotations.

Camporesi, Piero. *The Fear of Hell: Images of Damnation and Salvation in Early Modern Europe*. University Park, PA: Penn State University Press, 1991.
Cited as "Camporesi" in the text.

Conyers, A. J. *The Eclipse of Heaven: Rediscovering the Hope of a World Beyond*. Downers Grove, IL: InterVarsity Press, 1992.
Cited as "Conyers" in the text.

Hambrick-Stowe, Charles. *The Practice of Piety: Puritan Devotional Disciplines in Seventeenth Century New England*. Chapel Hill, NC: UNC Press, 1983.
Cited as "Hambrick-Stowe" in the text.

Marsden, George. *Jonathan Edwards: A Life*. New Haven: Yale Univ. Press, 2003.
Cited as "Marsden" in the text.

Marten, James. *Children in Colonial America*. New York: NYU Press, 2006.
Cited as "Marten" in the text.

Morgan, Christopher W. and Robert A. Peterson. *Hell Under Fire: Modern Scholarship Reinvents Eternal Punishment.* Grand Rapids: Zondervan, 2004.
Cited as "Hell Under Fire" in the text.

Norton Anthology of American Literature, vol. 1. New York: W. W. Norton & Company, 1979.
Cited as "Norton" in the text.

Walker, D. P. *Decline of Hell: Seventeenth-Century Discussions of Eternal Torment.* Chicago: University of Chicago Press, 1964.
Cited as "Walker" in the text.

Wells, David. *Above All Earthly Pow'rs: Christ in a Postmodern World.* Grand Rapids: Eerdmans, 2005.
Cited as "Wells" in the text.

Website

http://www.barna.org/barna-update/article/5-barna-update/128-americans-describe-their-views-about-life-after-death.
Cited as "Barna" in the text.

Books in the Yale University Press
Works of Jonathan Edwards series

In the text, the volumes are listed in the following format: (*Works* 1, 200). The "1" refers to the series volume; the "200" refers to the page number in the given volume.

Edwards, Jonathan. *The Great Awakening*, ed. C. C. Goen, *The Works of Jonathan Edwards*, vol. 4. New Haven: Yale, 1972.

_____. *Ethical Writings*, ed. Paul Ramsay, *The Works of Jonathan Edwards*, vol. 8. New Haven: Yale, 1989.

_____. *A History of the Work of Redemption*, ed. John F. Wilson, *The Works of Jonathan Edwards*, vol. 9. New Haven: Yale, 1989.

_____. *Sermons and Discourses, 1720–1723*, ed. Wilson H. Kimnach, *The Works of Jonathan Edwards*, vol. 10. New Haven: Yale, 1992.

_____. *Sermons and Discourses, 1723–1729*, ed. Kenneth E. Minkema, *The Works of Jonathan Edwards*, vol. 14. New Haven: Yale, 1997.

_____. *Letters and Personal Writings*, ed. George S. Claghorn, *The Works of Jonathan Edwards*, vol. 16. New Haven: Yale, 1998.

_____. *Sermons and Discourses, 1730–1733*, ed. Mark Valeri, *The Works of Jonathan Edwards*, vol. 17. New Haven: Yale, 1999.

_____. *Sermons and Discourses, 1734–1738*, ed. M. X. Lesser, *The Works of Jonathan Edwards*, vol. 19. New Haven: Yale, 2001.

_____. *Sermons and Discourses, 1739–1742*, ed. Harry S. Stout and Nathan O. Hatch with Kyle P. Farley, *The Works of Jonathan Edwards*, vol. 22. New Haven: Yale, 2003.

_____. *Sermons and Discourses, 1743–1758*, ed. Wilson H. Kimnach, *The Works of Jonathan Edwards*, vol. 25. New Haven: Yale, 2006.

Jonathan Edwards, a God-Entranced Man

*W*hen I was in seminary, a wise professor told me that besides the Bible I should choose one great theologian and apply myself throughout life to understanding and mastering his thought. This way I would sink at least one shaft deep into reality, rather than always dabbling on the surface of things. I might come to know at least one system with which to bring other ideas into fruitful dialogue. It was good advice.

The theologian I have devoted myself to is Jonathan Edwards. All I knew of Edwards when I went to seminary was that he preached a sermon called "Sinners in the Hands of an Angry God," in which he said something about hanging over hell by a slender thread. My first real encounter with Edwards was when I read his "Essay on the Trinity" and wrote a paper on it for church history.

It had a lasting effect on me. It gave me a conceptual framework with which to grasp, in part, the meaning of saying God is three in one. In brief, there is God the Father, the fountain of being, who from all eternity has had a perfectly clear and distinct image and idea of himself; and this image is the eternally begotten Son. Between this Son and Father there flows a stream of infinitely vigorous love and perfectly holy communion; and this is God the Spirit. God's Image of God and God's Love of God are so full of God that they are fully divine Persons, and not less.

After graduation from college, and before my wife and I took off for graduate work in Germany, we spent some restful days on a small farm in Barnesville, Georgia. Here I had another encounter with Edwards. Sitting on one of those old-fashioned two-seater swings in the backyard under a big hickory tree, with pen in hand, I read *The Nature of True Virtue*. I have a long entry in my journal from July 14, 1971, in which I try to understand, with Edwards's help, why a Christian is obligated to forgive wrongs when there seems to be a moral law in our hearts that cries out against evil in the world.

Later, when I was in my doctoral program in Germany, I encountered Edwards's *Dissertation Concerning the End for Which God Created the World*. I read it in a pantry in our little apartment in Munich. The pantry was about 8 by 5 feet, a most unlikely place to read a book like the *Dissertation*. From my perspective now, I would say that if there were one book that captures the essence or wellspring of Edwards's theology, this would be it. Edwards's answer to the question of why God created the world is this: to emanate the fullness of His glory for His people to know, praise, and enjoy. Here is the heart of his theology in his own words:

> IT APPEARS THAT ALL that is ever spoken of in the Scripture as an ultimate end of God's works is included in that one phrase, *the glory of God.* In the creatures' knowing, esteeming, loving, rejoicing in and praising God, the glory of God is both exhibited and acknowledged; his fullness is received and returned. Here is both the *emanation* and *remanation.* The refulgence shines upon and into the creature, and is reflected back to the luminary. The beams of glory come from God, and are something of God and are refunded back again to their original. So that the whole is *of* God and *in* God, and *to* God, and God is the beginning, middle and end in this affair. (Works 8, 531)

That is the heart and center of Jonathan Edwards and, I believe, of the Bible too. That kind of reading can turn a pantry into a vestibule of heaven.

I am not the only person for whom Edwards continues to be a vestibule of heaven. I hear testimonies regularly that people have stumbled upon this man's work and had their world turned upside down. There are simply not many writers today whose mind and heart are God-entranced the way Edwards was. Again and again, to this very day his writings help me know that experience.

My prayer for *The Essential Edwards Collection* is that it will draw more people into the sway of Edwards's God-entranced worldview. I hope that many who start here, or continue here, will make their way to Edwards himself. Amazingly, almost everything he wrote is available on the Internet. And increasingly his works are available in affordable books. I am thankful that Owen Strachan and Douglas Sweeney share my conviction that every effort to point to Edwards, and through him to his God, is a worthy investment of our lives. May that be the outcome of these volumes.

John Piper
Pastor for Preaching and Vision
Bethlehem Baptist Church
Minneapolis, Minnesota

Edwards and the Reality of the Afterlife

*T*he question of the afterlife is, for many today, one of preference. Christians trained to evangelize unsaved people with the question, "If you were to die today, do you know where you would go—heaven or hell?" are sometimes perplexed when met with the response, "I don't believe in heaven or hell." Heard once, this answer fails to deter us; heard twice, we began to wonder what's up; heard a dozen times, we realize that something in our culture had changed. The ground has shifted beneath our feet.

It was not always so. In fact, in most parts of the world in most eras of history, people had little clue that they could conveniently opt out of an eschatological (or eternity-focused) life. The Christian worldview, for centuries the most popular system of belief in the West, posited the existence of two realms, heaven and hell, which received either the eternally saved or the eternally lost, respectively. Though belief has waxed and waned over the last two millennia, most people have stared the reality of these two realms in the face. For most people of the past, mortality was not a distant prospect, one that could be pushed off for years, even decades. It was a constant reality. Whether they wanted to or not, most people had to confront death and the afterlife on a regular basis, whether from life circumstances or from religious instruction.

It is the purpose of this book to reacquaint modern Christians and other interested readers with the eschatologically driven preaching and teaching of Jonathan Edwards. This word "eschatological" may trip some readers up at first encounter, but as noted above, it refers simply to "last things," things of eternity and ultimate significance. This volume will present Edwards's material on the reality of the afterlife, the terror of hell, the glories of heaven, and the shape life must take in light of these truths. In doing so, it will illuminate the depth and richness of Edwards's thinking on the afterlife.

We interact extensively in *Jonathan Edwards on Heaven and Hell* with the actual writing of Edwards. It will take a little time to get used to his style, but it is our belief that investing even a little effort in reading his writing will yield a huge spiritual payoff. We will mix in our commentary on his writing even as we sketch a general picture of his understanding of heaven and hell. As we go, we will offer brief suggestions for application of his views that we hope will be of use to you in your personal reading or in the context of group study.

Though we both enjoy delving deeply into subjects like this one, we cannot cover every base in this book. The broader *Essential Edwards Collection* allows the reader to delve much deeper into Edwards's thinking and preaching, but we seek in *Jonathan Edwards on Heaven and Hell* to bring to light an important emphasis of Edwards's ministry, one that few may recognize but all can profit from. We aim here to make Edwards accessible to a wide audience. This book is intended for the uninitiated, but we hope and intend for it—and for this series—to be of use to pastors, students, church leaders, small groups, and many more besides. We want both Edwards's self-proclaimed "homeboys" as well as total strangers to his material to enjoy and benefit from his deeply inspiring teaching.

It is our hope that this little book will contribute to a renaissance of belief in things of eternal significance. As we will explore in chapter 1, it is hard for us to believe in an afterlife today, and especially difficult for us to believe in the afterlife as Scripture presents it. Yet if we will accept the Word as our authority, and if we will allow Edwards to serve as our faithful and visionary guide, we will find that God is alive. He is the Lord of heaven and earth, the sovereign ruler of all Creation. Though many attempt to silence the Lord, He is not silent. His revelation on the afterlife demands our attention, our concern, and our whole-hearted worship and trust.

CHAPTER ONE

The Disappearance of the Afterlife

THOSE–DYING THEN,
Knew where they went—
They went to God's Right Hand—
That Hand is amputated now
And God cannot be found—

The abdication of Belief
Makes the Behavior small—
Better an ignis fatuus
Than no illume at all—

(Norton, 2383)

*J*onathan Edwards did not write these words. They were composed by Emily Dickinson. Dickinson, one of America's greatest poets of the nineteenth century, wrote the brief and untitled poem in a different cultural climate than Edwards's. The American colonies had become a nation. The Industrial Revolution had transformed daily life. Most pertinent to the poem, many pastors had embraced the popular academic spirit that effectively deemphasized the historic doctrines of orthodox Christianity.

The Christian faith as experienced by many church members had changed, too. Where Christians had once emphasized in the glories of heaven and the terrors of hell, many professing believers in Dickinson's era suffered an apparent "abdication of Belief." They no longer subscribed to the awesome truths of immortality. Instead, they busied themselves with the things of this world. Dickinson, though not an avid churchgoer herself, lamented this situation and the impoverished moral behavior it produced.

The same problem that Dickinson observed many years ago belongs to our age. Many believers and churches do not reflect deeply on the age to come. Evangelicalism as a whole seems to have shifted focus from the life to come to life in this world. This has the unfortunate consequence of diminishing the importance of ultimate realities.

The call to preach the need for salvation and the prospect of the afterlife proceeds from the Scripture. In one section from the book of Ezekiel, the Lord thunders to Ezekiel, His prophet, to do just this, warning him of the dire consequences of failure on this point:

> SO YOU, SON OF MAN, I have made a watchman for the house of Israel. Whenever you hear a word from my mouth, you shall give them warning from me. If I say to the wicked, O wicked one, you shall surely die, and you do not speak to warn the wicked to turn from his way, that wicked person shall die in his iniquity, but his blood I will require at your hand. But if you warn the wicked to turn from his way, and he does not turn from his way, that person shall die in his iniquity, but you will have delivered your soul. (Ezekiel 33:7–9)

Though the passage does not mention heaven and hell, it shows that the Lord holds His shepherds and prophets responsible for declaring His message of salvation. The prophets were divinely called to warn the people of God of the reality of judgment and the need to reconcile themselves to their Creator and Judge. The prophet did not choose whether or not to highlight these things. The people, for their part, were not free to pick and choose which parts of the prophet's message they liked best.

Much has changed since Ezekiel's day, when every person could not help but come face to face with both their mortality and the truth of the afterlife. We feel this shift keenly in the West, where various factors push against the biblical teaching on the afterlife. In the broader culture, hell, especially, is a relic of a severe past, an idea that few people seriously entertain. Heaven, on the other hand, retains popularity, though what heaven actually looks like in the minds of many has changed dramatically. In Christian circles, though many believers retain belief in heaven and hell, the practical reality is that this earth often has more significance for many of us than does the afterlife.

To begin to rectify this situation, we must first understand how we have arrived at this place. We will do so in this first chapter. We will briefly tour our cultural history, examining how belief in the afterlife has changed and decreased over the last few centuries. After we have traced the decline of belief in the afterlife, we will turn to the writing and thinking of Jonathan Edwards in pursuit of a biblical eschatological vision. The colonial New England pastor-theologian devoted a great deal of attention to the afterlife and penned numerous pieces that called for his audience to reckon with the prospect of eternity in either heaven or hell. These pieces, whether sermons to his congregation, theological treatises, or letters to his children, illustrate his convictions and will revive our own. Through study of them, we will see that Edwards wrote and preached on the need to prepare one's soul for death not because he was a killjoy, but because he loved his people deeply and wanted them to avoid wrath and taste eternal life.

A Brief Cultural History
of Belief in the Afterlife

Our remarks on this point can only be brief as we provide a sketch of the decline of belief in hell in our society. As we will see, the story of widespread loss of faith in the afterlife parallels the larger story of cultural unbelief.

As noted in the introduction, the vast majority of people in the history of the world believed in a dualistic afterlife. For much of the last two millennia in the West, Catholicism and Protestantism have held sway over the minds and hearts of the common people. Though these two strands of Christianity have significant differences, each has traditionally taught that heaven and hell exist. Taking this teaching from the Bible, church leaders passed it on to their followers, who in turn accepted the teaching as truth. They had no perception as many of us do that they were choosing one worldview option among many. Rather, the biblical teaching as mediated by their church leaders was fact, and they were required by God to believe His Word.

Popular views of hell in the Middle Ages, for example, were often visceral and horrifying, far removed from our sanitized modern conceptions, as historian Piero Camporesi shows:

THE "SEPULCHRE OF HELL", "with its fetid corpses which were indissolubly linked to hundreds of others", this "rubbish heap of rotting matter devours the dead without disintegrating them, disintegrates them without incinerating them, and incinerates them in everlasting death", worked like a peculiar self-feeding incinerator which simultaneously disintegrated and regenerated the rubbish which flowed from the rotten world, and paradoxically transformed the ephemeral into immortal, elevating the rejects and garbage into eternal, glorious trophies of divine justice. It was like a "rubbish heap filled with little worms" whose contents are continually regenerated and reintegrated in an incomprehensible cycle of sublimated destruction. (Camporesi, 55)

Pictures like this played in the minds of the masses for ages. Unlike our era, when many Christians shut hell from their minds, in previous days most people would have heard sermons illustrating the horrors of the realm of the damned.

Everything began to change in the sixteenth, seventeenth, and eighteenth centuries, however. Some thinkers, following trends begun in the Renaissance, began to openly question the authority of the Bible, the existence of God, and the reality of heaven and hell. In Europe, especially in influential France, the number of "heretics" swelled as highly intelligent philosophers—called "philosophes"—launched attacks against the dogma of the Catholic Church. The Church, not used to having its teaching questioned so boldly in public, reacted strongly against the philosophes, which won the thinkers great approval from their peers. In time, through the power of the printing press, the Enlightenment's ideas spread from country to country and city to city.

As history shows, the Enlightenment accomplished nothing less than a sea change in the West. Coupled with factors like rising health standards and increased social prosperity due to the rise of markets, many common folk began to wonder whether Christianity was worth all the moral trouble, with all of its constraints and denunciations, and whether heaven and hell might be little more than an invention of the church. Camporesi vividly describes this shift:

> TOGETHER WITH THE GROWING infrequency of famine and the extinction of that other divine punishment, the plague, the European desire for life, which was reflected in the demographic increase and the rebirth of Christian hope in the form of a less absolute and tyrannical, less cruel and severe justice, laid the foundations, under the long influence of rationalism, for deism, pantheism, and for an anti-dogmatic historical criticism and skepticism; it even led to the dismantling of the dark city of punishment and to the gradual emptying—through the filter of a deliberate mental reform—of the life—prison of the damned. (Camporesi, 103–4)

The teaching of the Enlightenment philosophers caused many people to question beliefs long established as truth, even as changing living conditions allowed people to gradually liberate themselves from other-worldly teachings. Freshly emboldened, many people distanced themselves from Christianity and its view of the afterlife in the eighteenth and nineteenth centuries. In the academy, which grew especially strong in the nineteenth century, higher criticism of the Bible caught on, and soon scholars were debunking whole books of the sacred text. It became fashionable among leading thinkers to disbelieve the Bible. Yet, this was by no means the only religious trend of this period; Christian revivals broke out frequently and Baptists and Methodists surged in popularity in this age. Even in Europe, stories of the demise of Christianity were in places greatly exaggerated. Yet a shift had taken place, one that altered the West for good.

We also need to look specifically at what has happened in America in the last 200 years to erode belief in the Christian afterlife. Theologian Al Mohler notes that in the nineteenth century in America, "Deists and Unitarians had rejected the idea of God as judge. In certain circles, higher criticism had undermined confidence in the Bible as divine revelation, and churchmen increasingly treated hell as a metaphor" (*Hell Under Fire*, 24–25). A new wing of Christianity rose to prominence in America in this time. Liberal Christianity explicitly retained certain elements of Christian teaching while rejecting others, including belief in an errorless Scripture, a wrathful God, a substitute sacrifice paying the blood penalty for sin, and hell. These views spread from New England—once the bastion of biblical Christianity in America—to various corners of the country, including many cities and centers of academic life.

The seed of doubt planted in the nineteenth century yielded a forest of skepticism in the twentieth. Mohler weighs in incisively:

> THEOLOGICALLY, THE CENTURY that began in comfortable Victorian eloquence quickly became fertile ground for nihilism and *angst*. What World War I did not destroy, World War II took by assault and atrocity. The battlefields of Verdun and Ypres gave way to the ovens of Dachau and Auschwitz as symbols of the century.
>
> At the same time, the technological revolutions of the century extended the worldview of scientific naturalism throughout much of the culture of the West, especially among elites. The result was a complete revolution in the place of religion in general, and Christianity in particular, in the public space. Ideological and symbolic secularization became the norm in Western societies with advanced technologies and ever-increasing levels of economic wealth. Both heaven and hell took on an essentially this-worldly character. (*Hell Under Fire*, 26)

The specter of secularism assaulted Christianity on numerous fronts, as the above makes clear. The great wars of the first part of the twentieth century swept away the tenuous Christian commitment of many Europeans and Americans. Weakened Christianity, Christianity without an omnipotent and all-wise God, a glorious Savior laying His life down to save His people, and eternal life and death, proved no match for the "ovens of Dachau and Auschwitz." Horror at the scope and spectacle of human suffering overwhelmed loosely held religious commitment.

With little connection to the rock-solid biblical foundation that nurtures the soul and buttresses the mind, modern man searched for a salve, a worldview that could give solace in the midst of mass destruction. His quest led him to various outlets. He found some relief in technology and the promise of scientific discovery. He nursed his spiritual wounds in the burgeoning psychological movement. He gave himself over to nihilism. He spent himself in hedonistic excess. In each of these outlets, he embraced a world-centered ideology and lost sight of the wonder of heaven and the horror of hell. Man, a spiritual creature bearing the imprint of eternity, morphed into a soulless being with no attachment to a concrete afterlife.

The Christian faith has suffered in the wake of these developments. Many Christian leaders have allowed the major cultural trends to shape the way they think about and live the Christian faith. Mohler suggests that in our day:

> SIN HAS BEEN REDEFINED as a lack of self–esteem rather than as an insult to the glory of God. Salvation has been reconceived as liberation from oppression, internal or external. The gospel becomes a means of release from bondage to bad habits rather than rescue from a sentence of eternity in hell. (*Hell Under Fire*, 40)

Historian D. P. Walker concurs in his treatment of the modern view of hell:

> ETERNAL TORMENT IS NOWADAYS an unpopular doctrine among most kinds of Christians; the God of love has nearly driven out the God of vengeance; vindictive justice has had to take refuge among the advocates of hanging; and it is no longer considered respectable to enjoy the infliction of even the justest punishment. (Walker, 262)

Philosopher A. J. Conyers points out that heaven is also out of vogue today:

> WE LIVE IN A WORLD no longer under heaven. At least in most people's minds and imaginations that vision of reality has become little more than a caricature, conjuring up the saints and angels of baroque frescoes. And in the church only a hint remains of the power it once exercised in the hearts of believers. (Conyers, 11)

The Christian church is losing its grasp on heaven and hell. As is clear from this testimony, when set against our fast-paced, ever-changing, self-serving world, the afterlife—seemingly so vague and far off—struggles to hold our attention.

What Moderns Believe about the Afterlife

Many who do believe in Christianity have modernized it. We have made our faith about fulfillment and achievement, sentimentalized love, and earthly progress. We have adopted the consumerist mind-set endemic to the West and have substituted the pursuit of plenty for the pursuit of piety. David Wells suggests:

> THIS EXPERIENCE OF ABUNDANCE which is the result of both extraordinary ingenuity and untamed desire is a tell-tale sign that we have moved from a traditional society to one that is modern, from a time when God and the supernatural were "natural" parts of life, to one in which God is now alienated and dislocated from our modernized world. In traditional societies, what one could legitimately have wanted was limited. It was, of course, limited because people lived with only a few choices and little knowledge of life other than the life they lived; their vision of life had not been invaded, as ours is, by pictures of beguiling Caribbean shorelines, sleek luxury under the Lexus insignia, time-shares in fabulous places, or exotic perfumes sure to stir hidden passions. (Wells, 42)

Wells's analysis brings us back to where we started: preference. We modern folk live with a mind-boggling array of choices that our ancestors never knew. The family's in Dallas, but do we prefer the weather in Denver? Our parents ran a drug store, but would we prefer dentistry? Should we have kids now, or delay five or six years? Would we like to reinvent our bodies? If so, what would we like to change—a new nose? Different eyelids? Fuller, thicker lips? In these and countless other ways—many of them neutral, a good number of them acceptable, and some of them downright harmful—we encounter the category of choice, never realizing how differently we act and think from our forebears.

When it comes to choices about the afterlife, Americans exercise their "right" with aplomb. A recent Barna poll probing belief in heaven and hell discovered the following results:

IN ALL, 76% BELIEVE that Heaven exists, while nearly the same proportion said that there is such a thing as Hell (71%). Respondents were given various descriptions of Heaven and asked to choose the statement that best fits their belief about Heaven. Those who believe in Heaven were divided between describing Heaven as "a state of eternal existence in God's presence" (46%) and those who said it is "an actual place of rest and reward where souls go after death" (30%). Other Americans claimed that Heaven is just "symbolic" (14%), that there is no such thing as life after death (5%), or that they are not sure (5%).

While there is no dominant view of Hell, two particular perspectives are popular. Four out of ten adults believe that Hell is "a state of eternal separation from God's presence" (39%) and one-third (32%) says it is "an actual place of torment and suffering where people's souls go after death." A third perspective that one in eight adults believe is that "Hell is just a symbol of an unknown bad outcome after death" (13%). Other respondents were "not sure" or said they that they do not believe in an afterlife (16%). (Barna)

These numbers reflecting belief in the afterlife may seem high given the foregoing commentary, and it is surely true that some form of belief in heaven and hell does persist today. Yet one cannot help but note the uncertainty when respondents attempted to define their views of hell. This is, after all, where the rubber meets the eschatological road. Many will profess to believe in Christian doctrine, but we must look closely at how they define this doctrine to grasp the strength of their belief. At the end of the day, far fewer people than one might think claim belief in heaven and hell as the Bible defines these realms. In addition, we might also note that one cannot separate heaven and hell, as so many seem to think. The Scripture does not give us the option of choosing which realm we want to believe in.

How a Loss of Biblical Belief in the Afterlife Has Affected the Church

The shifts in cultural thinking about the afterlife have transformed the way many Christians preach. Many pastors wish to reach people for Jesus, but they know that many folks have little patience with heady doctrine or biblical instruction. They choose to preach on more practical matters, areas that most people can readily understand. This kind of approach is understandable, but it has the unfortunate effect of silencing what past Christians have called the "whole counsel" of God, meaning the full sweep of biblical theology. In this kind of environment, preaching can become little more than an advice session or what others have called "group therapy."

Many pastors resist these trends. But where they do not, the people in the pew have little stimulus to think about the afterlife and things of eternal consequence. We are left instead to think much about things of this world. Thus, many of us think little about heaven and a good deal about football, renovating our houses, shopping, or gossip. We rarely talk about hell but often about television and movies. We joke about being "heavenly minded" and shy away from Christians who seem to be, viewing them as odd and out-of-place (indeed, they are). We strive to be cool, hip, fashionable, relevant, and plugged in, unaware of how little these things will matter in eternity. Our mind-set, unbeknownst to us, is almost entirely rooted in this world. We have little connection with the life to come, which the Scripture teaches has already begun in us and in our churches (Mark 1:15).

Many of us sense this sad situation and want it to change. We do not want to be so busy, and we do not like what certain aspects of our modern way of life have done to our devotions, our daily thoughts, and our time at church. Many of us want to be more focused on heaven and more faithful in leading people away from hell through gospel proclamation. The problem, though, is that our modern lifestyle has trained us only to think deeply and searchingly about things like heaven and hell when our more pressing concerns have ceased—which is a rare occurrence.

An Edwardsean Solution to Our Modern Dilemma

Though the task seems impossible, we have guides who have gone before us and who can help us to recover an eschatological perspective. One of them is the colonial pastor Jonathan Edwards, who devoted tremendous amounts of time and energy to thinking and teaching on heaven and hell. In chapters to come, we will look at Edwards's specific views, seeing how very real heaven and hell actually are, and finding our hearts stirred by the biblical material that Edwards powerfully exposits.

Having laid out the loss of our cultural connection with the afterlife, we're going to start our study with a look at how the afterlife was viewed in Edwards's own cultural context, as well as examine what Edwards said about the general subject of the afterlife and how he sought to cultivate a mind-set in his people that bound their lives to the age to come. We will look briefly at a number of different writings from the pastor that show just how concerned he was with the afterlife—and demonstrate how great our own interest must be.

Edwards's Cultural Context

In Edwards's eighteenth-century era, the afterlife dominated the thinking of many people, including parents, who sought to ready their children for their eternal destiny. Historian George Marsden describes how many parents prepared their children for death in his magisterial volume *Jonathan Edwards*:

> MUCH OF PURITAN UPBRINGING was designed to teach children to recognize how insecure their lives were. Every child knew of brothers, sisters, cousins, or friends who had suddenly died. Cotton Mather . . . eventually lost thirteen of his fifteen children. Parents nightly reminded their children that sleep was a type of death and taught them such prayers as "This day is past; but tell me who can say / That I shall surely live another day." . . . One of the Edwards children's surviving writing exercises reads, "Nothing is more certain than death. Take no delay in the great work of preparing for death." (Marsden, 26–7)

Popular literature of the day underscored this perspective. Historian Charles Hambrick-Stowe comments on a wildly successful author, Michael Wigglesworth, who wrote a popular book called *The Day of Doom:*

> WIGGLESWORTH EXHORTED thousands of New Englanders to prepare for death in *The Day of Doom* and his other poems. His prefatory lines explicitly stated that the epic's purpose was "That Death and Judgment may not come / And find thee unprepared." His overriding method in *The Day of Doom* was to instill the fear of Christ as terrible Judge and drive penitents to Him for mercy in this life before it was too late. Terror was a means of grace, but the hoped for end was escape from terror. "Oh get a part in Christ," Wigglesworth cried, "And make the Judge thy Friend." (Hambrick-Stowe, 239–40)

Such a text would struggle to find even a Christian publisher today, but colonial New England prized literature of a different kind, as Hambrick-Stowe's reports of sales records show: "*The Day of Doom* was the most popular piece of literature in seventeenth-century New England. An unprecedented eighteen-hundred copies were printed in the first edition in 1662, which sold out in the first year. Thereafter the work was reissued repeatedly" (Hambrick-Stowe, 240).

We might wonder what cultural impulse accounted for these hefty sales figures. Colonial citizens of the seventeenth and eighteenth centuries knew a world much different from ours. They had no hospitals. They possessed precious few working remedies for illness. They knew very little about the causes of sickness—germ theory, for example, did not emerge until the mid-nineteenth century. Pregnancy and labor were potentially fearful undertakings: scholars have estimated that one in six children died in colonial America, meaning that most families would mourn the loss of at least one or two children in their lifetime (Marten, 80). Attacks from Native Americans posed a constant threat in many places. American colonists did not study death out of a perverse fascination, but practical necessity. Where we try to cheat death, they prepared themselves to meet death.

Edwards's Focus on the Afterlife

As was common for a minister of his time, Edwards often confronted death in his preaching. For example, in his sermon "The Importance of a Future State," he discoursed plainly about death, reminding his people of its certain visitation:

> BUT ALL OTHER MEN must die in the ordinary way of separation of their souls from their bodies. Men of all ranks, degrees, and orders must die: strong [and] weak; kings, princes [and] beggars; rich [and] poor; good [and] bad. (*Works* 10, 356–7)

Edwards outlined how God had planted eternity in the heart of all people, leaving us with the knowledge in our conscience that this life is not the end of things. He wrote:

> NOW GOD HAS IMPLANTED in us this natural disposition of expecting a reward or punishment, according as we do well or ill, for this disposition is natural to us: 'tis in our very nature; God had made it with us. And to what purpose should God make in us a disposition to expect rewards and punishments if there are none? (*Works* 10, 357)

Edwards had a plainspoken approach to death and the life beyond. Death, for him, was a fundamental consequence of existence. All people must face it. Accordingly, Edwards sought to prepare his people for the end.

In another sermon, "Death and Judgment," preached to his Native American congregation in Stockbridge, the pastor walked his listeners through the essential matters of life and death:

> IN THIS WORLD, sometimes, wicked men are great kings, and deal very hardly and cruelly with good men, and put 'em to death; and therefore, there must be another world where good men shall all be happy and wicked men miserable. . . .
>
> In another world, God will call 'em to an account [of] what they have done here in this world: how they have

improved their time, and whe[ther] they have kept his com-
mandments or no.

He will [hold] them to an account that have heard the
gospel preached; [he will ask] whether or no they have
repented of their sins and have in their hearts accepted of
Jesus Christ as their Savior.

And then all wicked men, and they that would not
repent of their sins and come [to] Christ, will have their
mouths stopped and will have nothing to say. (*Works* 25,
594–95)

The pastor's straightforward approach to the afterlife allowed
him to reach his Native American audience in clear, understandable language. Sermons like this one revealed how the
decisions and habits of this life had far-reaching consequences for the next. In the afterlife God would balance the
scales of justice.

The pastor's sermons on the afterlife took many forms,
some plain, others soaring in their sweep. In his "Farewell
Sermon" to his Northampton congregation, Edwards painted
a hair-raising picture of the last day that surely grabbed the
attention of his hearers:

ALTHOUGH THE WHOLE WORLD will be then present, all
mankind of all generations gathered in one vast assembly,
with all of the angelic nature, both elect and fallen angels;
yet we need not suppose, that everyone will have a distinct

and particular knowledge of each individual of the whole
assembled multitude, which will undoubtedly consist of
many millions of millions. Though 'tis probable that men's
capacities will be much greater than in their present state,
yet they will not be infinite: though their understanding
and comprehension will be vastly extended, yet men will
not be deified. There will probably be a very enlarged view,
that particular persons will have of the various parts and
members of that vast assembly. . . . There will be special
reason, why those who have had special concerns together
in this world, in their state of probation, and whose mutual
affairs will be then to be tried and judged, should especially be set in one another's view.

The last day would mark the end of man's ability to repent.
When all people appeared before the great judgment seat of
God, none could change their stripes, a fact that Edwards
brought out in chilling detail:

> BUT WHEN THEY SHALL MEET together at the day of judg-
> ment . . . they will all meet in an unchangeable state. Sin-
> ners will be in an unchangeable state: they who then shall
> be under the guilt and power of sin, and have the wrath of
> God abiding on them, shall be beyond all remedy or pos-
> sibility of change, and shall meet their ministers without
> any hopes of relief or remedy, or getting any good by their

means. And as for the saints, they will be already perfectly delivered from all their before-remaining corruption, temptation and calamities of every kind, and set forever out of their reach; and no deliverance, no happy alteration will remain to be accomplished in the way of the use of means of grace, under the administration of ministers. It will then be pronounced, "He that is unjust, let him be unjust still; and he that is filthy, let him be filthy still; and he that is righteous, let him be righteous still; and he that is holy, let him be holy still" [Revelation 22:11]. (*Works* 25, 466)

With his exegetical insight and vivid imagination, Edwards transported his hearers to the holy ground he described. Behind his foreboding sketch of the day of judgment was a pressing concern that his people prepare themselves for it. Edwards closed his sermon with a hopeful but sober call to seek the Lord while He could be found as a Savior and not a Judge:

DEAR CHILDREN, I leave you in an evil world, that is full of snares and temptations. God only knows what will become of you. This the Scripture has told us, that there are but few saved: and we have abundant confirmation of it from what we see. This we see, that children die as well as others: multitudes die before they grow up; and of those that grow up, comparatively few ever give good evidence of saving conversion to God. I pray God to pity you, and take care of you, and provide for you the best means for the good of your souls; and that God himself would undertake for you, to be your heavenly Father, and the mighty Redeemer of your immortal souls. (*Works* 25, 484–5)

The pastor's final words to the Northampton congregation did not resolve the bitter conflict between Edwards and his detractors. They did, however, direct the church members to recognize the fragility of life and to throw themselves on the mercy of Christ.

Edwards did not only preach this message to his congregation. He spoke of it constantly to his children. To live in the Edwards household was to come into regular contact with the reality of death and the necessity of gospel preparation for the afterlife. The following letter to Edwards's daughter Esther, dated May 27, 1755, shows both the tenderness and seriousness of the father on these matters. It is worth quoting at length:

DEAR CHILD,

Though you are a great way off from us, yet you are not out of our minds: I am full of concern for you, often think of you, and often pray for you. Though you are at so great a distance from us, and from all your relations, yet this is a comfort to us, that the same God that is here, is also at Onohquaga; and that though you are out of our sight and out of our reach, you are always in God's hands, who is infinitely gracious; and we can go to him, and commit you to his care and mercy. Take heed that you don't forget or neglect him. Always set God before your eyes, and live in his fear, and seek him every day with all diligence: for 'tis he, and he only can make you happy or miserable, as he pleases; and your life and health, and the eternal salvation of your soul, and your all in this life and that which is to come, depends on his will and pleasure.

The week before last, on Thursday, David died; whom you knew and used to play with, and who used to live at our house. His soul is gone into the eternal world. Whether he was prepared for death, we don't know. This is a loud call of God to you to prepare for death. You see that they that are young die, as well as those that are old: David was not very much older than you. Remember what Christ has said, that you must be born again, or you never can see the kingdom of God. Never give yourself any rest, unless you have good evidence that you are converted and become a new creature. We hope that God will preserve your life and health, and return you to Stockbridge again in safety; but always remember that life is uncertain: you know not how soon you must die, and therefore had need to be always ready.

We have very lately heard from your brothers and sisters at
Northampton and at Newark, that they are well. Your aged
grandfather and grandmother, when I was at Windsor, gave
their love to you. We here all do the same.

> I am,
>
> Your tender and affectionate father,
>
> Jonathan Edwards.
>
> (*Works* 16, 666–67)

The letter makes clear both that Jonathan took eternity very
seriously and that he loved his daughter Esther. He expressed
that he was "full of concern" for her, and his tone is affec-
tionate throughout. But sentimentality did not overwhelm
theology for Edwards. Love at its height involved concern for
the soul and ultimate things. Edwards thus went to great
lengths to impress upon his little girl that she needed to
"always set God before" her if she was to transcend this life
and rest eternally with Him in heaven. Surely, she had
received many letters and admonitions just like this one. In
his fathering, as in his preaching, Edwards communicated
that death was close—but so was the God of mercy.

Rediscovering the Afterlife

In our age, the worldviews of too many Christians resem-
ble the nineteenth-century system of belief so eloquently
decried in the poem by Emily Dickinson quoted in the intro-

duction. In our day, many of us busy ourselves with this world and the perfection of our existence in it. We have little fire for an otherworldly lifestyle, because we have little connection to the other world. It is generally taken for granted, rarely meditated on, rarely spoken of. The temporality of this life, the fragility of it, is forgotten.

Hope does exist for a recovery of vigorous spiritual belief and practice. In the work and example of Edwards and many other eternity-minded Christians from the past, we find the perspective we need. Edwards lived and worked as if heaven and hell were real, because he knew that they were. Our contact with Edwards's vivid, biblically saturated descriptions of the day of judgment and the age to come chart the way forward. We need to let the biblical testimony on the afterlife seep into our consciences and steep for a while so that we may pursue a new way of thinking and living.

In a world stricken with a plague of narcissism and distractedness, it is essential that we recognize the truth about the afterlife now, while we may ready ourselves for the end. Death and the final judgment swiftly approach us all. In these last days, our only hope is to prepare ourselves for the end by seeking the one who holds eternity in His mighty hand.

Preparing for Eternity

Know How the World Is Shaping Your Thoughts

*I*n an age when many ignore or disdain the Bible's teaching on eternity, the challenge for Christians is to both believe the truth about eternity and then to live in light of it. We may accomplish the first by studying scriptural books like the Minor Prophets, which have much to say about the judgment and the afterlife, the Pauline epistles (1 and 2 Thessalonians, for example), and the book of Revelation. As we study these works with a commentary at hand to help us puzzle through the hard parts, we can also immerse ourselves in strong theology. As one can readily tell, the work of Jonathan Edwards is a great place to start. The Puritans of post-Reformation era England and America focused a great deal on the afterlife (the Puritan paperbacks from Banner of Truth books have much helpful material on this subject). This kind of self-education will help us to refute unsound thinking even as it expands our own worldview and stokes our imagination to contemplate the life to come.

This last point is worth pondering. Though we need to steer clear of emotional speculation, it will do us great good to think about heaven by using our imaginations in accordance with the Bible. The Scripture is a visionary book, one that engages our minds, fires our thoughts, and rouses us to action. It is not a tame book. It will swallow us whole, transforming our understanding of this world and the next. If we do not let the biblical testimony on heaven and hell play in our minds, it will surely rest lightly on our hearts, causing us to lose sight of the monumental vision the Lord gave us of the age to come.

Know How the World Is Shaping Your Deeds

*O*nce we have begun this theological work, we will find that our spiritual lives change. We will be able to identify where Satan and this world have tricked us into living as if this realm matters more than eternity. We will surely see that we have disobeyed the teaching of 1 John 2:15 (a great verse on which to meditate) and have loved the things of this world too much. Our specific sins on this point will vary, but many of us will see that instead of living according to biblically determined priorities, we have in many ways mimicked our secular counterparts and loved possessions and this-worldly experiences more than we should have.

This mindset shows at numerous points in our lives. It has affected our parenting, causing us, at times, to postpone family devotions and close shepherding for another day. Many of us struggle to keep work in proper balance. We are tempted to sacrifice valuable time with our families, friends, and fellow church members for the sake of a few corruptible possessions. Everywhere around us are people with eternal souls, and yet many of us have difficulty beginning evangelistic friendships.

We support missionaries in principle, but sometimes we give more support to the local mall or golf club than to the work of the gospel.

In these and many other ways, the world is causing us to prioritize it and not God. The gospel is meant to usher in an eschatological life, a life lived with heaven and hell in full view. This life will naturally include many of the good things common to this world, but it has a fundamentally different orientation and frame of reference than the unbelieving life, which is by definition this-worldly. Our challenge, then, is plain—we need to take heaven and hell seriously. We need to glorify God by prioritizing eternity. We need to show the world by the way we live that heaven and hell are real. Belief in the afterlife is not, as so many think, a matter of preference. It is a necessity with eternal consequences. This point will only make sense to unbelievers around us when we Christians, those who have been claimed for all eternity, live with the reality of eternity ever before us.

CHAPTER TWO

The Frightening Prospect of Hell

*T*he movie scene is familiar to many of us today. A small figure struggles across a craggy landscape, fighting the force of an evil will as he goes. Accompanied by a trustworthy companion, he follows the lead of an unlikely guide, a strange creature of unearthly skin tone. The figure, of course, is Frodo Baggins, and the story is *The Lord of the Rings*, derived from the book series by J. R. R. Tolkien.

The story of this film centers around Frodo's quest for Mordor, the city of evil and death, ruled over by the spirit of Sauron, the dark lord. Though *Lord of the Rings* is just a movie, it conveys a sense of terrible dread. Mordor is a force for evil, a place of destruction and malevolence, and it is sheer madness for Frodo and his party to approach it. In this cinematic locale, we get a taste of what a realm of darkness might be like. Outside of frightening films, most of us rarely encounter, let alone mull over, such places of suffering and torment. For most people in the broader culture, the hellish place that is Mordor is nothing more than the outworkings of a particularly active imagination.

There is truth to this thought. However, Mordor is based on a real place. Not a place on this earth, of course, but a realm far beyond this world, known to students of the Bible as hell. The Scripture offers a description of a hell that makes Mordor seem tame by comparison. Led by Jesus, who spoke more than any other single figure about hell, the biblical voices present this realm as a real place where the unrepentant sinner is punished eternally for his sins.

Among eminent preachers of the Christian past, Jonathan Edwards represents an unparalleled guide to the doctrine of hell. This chapter will examine several of Edwards's sermons that consider hell with great depth, insight, and clarity. These include "Warnings of Future Punishment Don't Seem Real to the Wicked," which shows us the dire predicament of the lost mind; *Distinguishing Marks of a Work of the Spirit of God*, which offers a stirring call to preach judgment; "The Torments of Hell Are Exceeding Great" and "Sinners in the Hands of an Angry God," which together offer an apocalyptic picture of hell; and "The Justice of God in the Damnation of Sinners," which shows that God is just in His work of judgment.

This material, taken together, shows the modern reader

both the weight of God's judgment and the need to preach in an Edwardsean fashion. We study Edwards's words not out of curiosity, but necessity. In an age that hates or ignores the doctrine of hell, the church of Christ must recover belief in the doctrine and declare that belief to the world.

As we turn to study the words of Edwards, we would first urge the reader to search the Bible to see how often it discusses eternal punishment. In the Old Testament, consider especially Deuteronomy 32, Isaiah 66, and Daniel 12. In the New Testament, see Matthew 5, 10, 18, 23, Mark 9, Luke 12, John 5, Galatians 6, Ephesians 5, 2 Thessalonians 1, and Revelation 14 and 20. Even those who find the doctrine abhorrent and reject it will find that Edwards's views on the matter mirror the Bible's. If we consider the Edwardsean vision of hell frightening, we must know that we cannot begin to imagine what the actual reality is like.

Taking Hell Seriously

Edwards preached on numerous occasions about the reality of future judgment. It was not the singular emphasis of his career, but neither was it a doctrinal footnote. In his sermon "Warnings of Future Punishment Don't Seem Real to the Wicked," based on God's warning to Lot in Genesis 19:14, we find a sound starting point for our analysis of Edwardsean preaching on hell. Though a grave reality of earthly life, most people, Edwards suggested, thought little about it:

NOW THE GREATER PART of men have not a lively sensible apprehension of the wrath of God and of eternal punishment; it never was set before their eyes and brought into clear view. They have very little of a notion what the wrath of God is, and so it don't appear very terrible to them. They have but a faint dull idea of the misery of the damned: and that is the reason that, when they are told of it, it don't terrify them. It seems to them like a fable or a dream that makes very little impression upon their minds. (*Works* 14, 202)

Edwards was right in his day, and he is right in ours. Most people have not engaged in sustained and purposeful reflection on the doctrine of hell. Most have heard little about it. Even those who have come face to face with the doctrine have not had it "brought into clear view" by careful, probing teaching. The natural mind has little motivation to carefully consider the matter, and thus the little knowledge of hell that most people possess doesn't "terrify them" but rather seems more like "a fable or a dream" than a possible conclusion to earthly life.

This lack of attention blinded the lost to the facts about hell. First, said Edwards, the lost had little sense of how they would suffer in hell:

THEY HAN'T A SENSIBLE apprehension of the manner of their punishment. 'Tis a strange punishment that is appointed to the workers of iniquity: it will be a torment

inflicted after a new manner, in a way that they never experienced anything like it while they were here in this world.
And it is a punishment that wicked men have but a very
little notion of. They hear that the wrath of God will be
poured out upon them, but they don't know what that
pouring out of God's wrath is. They hear that there will be
horror of conscience, but they know but very little what
that horror of conscience will be. And therefore pouring
out of God's wrath, and horror of conscience, don't seem
very dreadful to them. They hear that they shall be tormented by devils, but they don't see how; and knowing but
little of the manner of the punishment, they ben't much
disquieted by fears of it. (*Works* 14, 203)

Unbelievers not only had no sense of how they would suffer
in eternity, they had no idea how overwhelming that suffering
would be:

THEY HAN'T A LIVELY sensible idea of the greatness of the
punishment. They hear that it will be intolerable, exceeding dreadful, that [it] will fill their souls with misery, that it
will be like fire and brimstone and the like; but they nevertheless seldom think what is meant by these expressions.
They never felt none of it, and never saw anybody under
this punishment or that ever did endure it, and so they
have no notion how dreadful it is—no, not of the hundredth

part of the greatness of that misery—and so they are not terrified and affrighted by it.

Furthermore, though they might have heard that judgment would last forever, they had no developed understanding of what eternal judgment would feel like:

> THEY HAVE NO LIVELY sensible apprehension of the eternity of this punishment. They consider but little, and apprehend but very little, what is meant by those words, "eternal," "everlasting," "forever and ever." They know but little what it will be to bear misery forever without change and without end. They don't imagine how it will be when they come to be in hell, to think with themselves, "Here I must be forever and ever; there is no escape; there is no help; there's no comfort." They have very little of an idea how such a despair will sink and oppress them, and will feel like a mountain of lead that will fall upon and crush them. (*Works* 14, 203)

In these passages, Edwards exposed the terrible plight of the unredeemed sinner. Those who reject the gospel have no sense, tragically, of what is coming for them. Even if they acknowledge that they deserve punishment for sin, it often doesn't "seem very dreadful to them." After they hear that hell will be dreadful beyond all comprehension, they still have "felt none of it" and "so they are not terrified" by it. Though they accept that hell is eternal, they "have little of an idea how such a despair," stretching over all the ages, will "fall upon and crush them."

In these ways, we see that the unregenerate mind-set opposes biblical logic. It makes no sense. It promises no hope. It makes things worse than they already are, because it leads the sinner to blithely refuse the truth and bury his head in the sand. The thinking of the natural man does not lead to life, to careful reflection on things that matter. It leads only to death.

Why Edwards Preached on Hell

Though the pastor did not often reflect on his reasons for preaching the doctrine of hell, he touched on his motivation in a brief section in his revival classic *The Distinguishing Marks of a Work of the Spirit of God.* His remarks inform the sermons covered in this chapter and instruct modern-day Christians on how to preach hell today.

In *Distinguishing Marks,* Edwards sought to help his fellow Christians think through the false and positive signs of a true work of God. In the course of doing so, he showed that it was folly not to preach about hell, for it was real and would claim every lost soul unless the truth was preached:

IF THERE BE REALLY a hell of such dreadful, and never-ending torments, as is generally supposed, that multitudes are in great danger of, and that the bigger part of men in Christian countries do actually from generation to generation fall into, for want of a sense of the terribleness of it, and their danger of it, and so for want of taking due care to avoid it; then why is it not proper for those that have the care of souls, to take great pains to make men sensible of it? Why should not they be told as much of the truth as can be? If I am in danger of going to hell, I should be glad to know as much as possibly I can of the dreadfulness of it: if I am very prone to neglect due care to avoid it, he does me the best kindness, that does most to represent to me the truth of the case, that sets forth my misery and danger in the liveliest manner. (*Works* 4, 246–47)

The treatment of the subject is straightforward and sensible. If hell is real, Edwards says, "I should be glad to know as much as possibly I can of the dreadfulness of it." The preacher knew that hell was real and thus viewed it as the "best kindness" to speak of it to lost souls. He felt fully justified in exposing humanity's "misery and danger in the liveliest manner." One did not simply state a sentence about hell and then move off of the subject as fast as possible. To do justice to the subject, one had to bring to light the full horror of the realm of the damned.

Edwards went on in *Distinguishing Marks* to underscore this approach to the subject by relating it to earthly situations of great danger:

I APPEAL TO EVERY ONE in this congregation, whether this is not the very course they would take in case of exposedness to any great temporal calamity? If any of you that are heads of families, saw one of your children in an house that was all on fire over its head, and in eminent danger of being soon consumed in the flames, that seemed to be very insensible of its danger, and neglected to escape, after you had often spake to it, and called to it, would you go on to speak to it only in a cold and indifferent manner? Would not you cry aloud, and call earnestly to it, and represent the danger it was in, and its own folly in delaying, in the most lively manner you was capable of? Would not nature itself teach this, and oblige you to it? If you should continue to speak to it only in a cold manner, as you are wont to do in ordinary conversation about indifferent matters, would not those about you begin to think you were bereft of reason yourself?

Even though this direct approach made great sense, few took note of its alarm, and fewer still heard it and then warned others of hell:

THIS IS NOT THE WAY of mankind, nor the way of any one person in this congregation, in temporal affairs of great moment, that require earnest heed and great haste, and about which they are greatly concerned, to speak to others of their danger, and warn them but a little; and when they do it at all, do it in a cold indifferent manner: nature teaches men otherwise. If we that have the care of souls, knew what hell was, had seen the state of the damned, or by any other means, become sensible how dreadful their case was; and at the same time knew that the bigger part of men went thither; and saw our hearers in eminent danger, and that they were not sensible of their danger, and so after being often warned neglected to escape, it would be morally impossible for us to avoid abundantly and most earnestly setting before them the dreadfulness of that misery they were in danger of, and their great exposedness to it, and warning them to fly from it, and even to cry aloud to them. (*Works* 4, 247)

The point is incontrovertible. When one has seen what hell is like through the testimony of the Scripture, one cannot help but warn others of hellfire. Man, contrary to what he often thinks, is not fine, but is "in eminent danger" that he is "not sensible" of. We who believe the Bible have not seen what hell actually is like, but we have read the New Testament's abundant coverage of it. We are thus called to tell the lost of their condition, to "cry aloud to them" and warn them of hell.

Edwards concluded his discussion of this matter in *Distinguishing Marks* by challenging those who failed to warn sinners of the hellish fate that awaited them. He contrasted their approach with his own:

SOME TALK OF IT as an unreasonable thing to think to fright persons to heaven; but I think it is a reasonable thing to endeavor to fright persons away from hell, that stand upon the brink of it, and are just ready to fall into it, and are senseless of their danger: 'tis a reasonable thing to fright a person out of an house on fire. The word "fright" is commonly used for sudden causeless fear, or groundless surprise; but surely a just fear, that there is good reason for, though it be very great, is not to be spoken against under any such name. (*Works* 4, 248)

Some in the pastor's day did not want to scare or "fright" people. Such preaching was "unreasonable." Yet Edwards, a man of academic distinction and refined sensibility, nonetheless knew that sinners stood "upon the brink" of hell. Though one's natural inhibitions might lead one to avoid scaring people, the certain danger of the sinner called Christians to warn them of their imminent fate. Though Edwards would not have endorsed scare tactics, he believed firmly in cultivating a "just fear," a proper biblical fright, of everlasting torment. Because so few people even thought about hell, the danger they faced was "very great." So too was the need for preaching on hellfire.

The logic of the matter required action. Edwards did not adopt his mind-set out of mere choice. He believed that he was obligated to tell the lost of their fate. Anything else would render him negligent and seal the damnation of his fellow man, who, instead of concerning himself with ultimate realities, busied himself with the small things of life. The Christian could not waste time. He could not waver about what to say. Judgment was real. Vengeance approached. The only hope of escape was true, vibrant, exhortational preaching on the darkness of hell and the liberating light of the gospel.

The Torments of Hell

Edwards went to great lengths in his preaching on hell to bring that realm of terror to life. In his sermon "The Torments of Hell Are Exceeding Great," based on Luke 16:24, Edwards walked his hearers through the theology of judgment, showing the foundations of the doctrine before leaving his audience with several pictures that made the discussion real.

Edwards began the sermon with a brief discussion of wrath. Wrath was not impersonal or abstract for Edwards. As a biblical Christian, he recognized that wrath was personal. It was God's own wrath:

THE PUNISHMENT THAT IS threatened to be inflicted on ungodly men is the wrath of God. God has often said that he will pour out his wrath upon the wicked. The wicked, they treasure up wrath; they are vessels of wrath, and they shall drink of the cup of God's wrath that is poured out without mixture. Revelation 14:10, "The same shall drink of the wine of the wrath of God, which is poured out without mixture." That is, there shall be no mixture of mercy; there shall be no sort of mitigation or moderation. God sometimes executes judgments upon sinners in this world, but it is with great mixtures of mercy and with restraint. But then there will be full and unmixed wrath. (*Works* 14, 304)

The pastor's words provide clarity on a subject that can easily drift into the abstract. Biblical wrath is not impersonal. It is the outpouring of the fury of a Person done wrong. From the first bite of the forbidden fruit to the present day, mankind has heaped up sins against God. Because of this, He will one day pour out His wrath, "full and unmixed," without mercy.

Edwards elaborated on the connection between God's character and His wrath, showing how numerous verses in Scripture showed Him to be angry at sin:

THE SCRIPTURE USES the same way of arguing to prove the dreadfulness of God's anger, from the greatness of his Being and majesty and power; and therefore we may be sure the argument is good. Psalms 90:11, "Who knoweth the power of thine anger? even according to thy fear, so is thy wrath." "According to thy fear"; that is, according to thy awful majesty and greatness, these fearful attributes. The Psalmist argues here from the greatness of God's majesty that the power of his anger is so great that we can't conceive of it. Again, Ezekiel 22:14, "Can thine heart endure, or can thine hands be strong, in the days that I shall deal with thee?" Where the argument is plainly this: that seeing 'tis God who shall deal with them, therefore their punishment will be intolerable. Again, 2 Thessalonians 1:7–9, "The Lord Jesus shall be revealed from heaven, in flaming fire taking vengeance on them who know not God, and obey not the gospel: who shall be punished with everlasting destruction from the presence of the Lord, and from the glory of his power." Where there is evidently an argument implied, that the punishment and destruction of unbelievers will be exceeding dreadful, because it comes from the presence of the Lord and because it is inflicted by such mighty power. Again, there is the same argument very plain, Hebrews 10:31, "It is a fearful thing to fall into the hands of the living God." (*Works* 14, 306)

Unbelievers sometimes express confidence in their ability to handle the judgment of God. Against such thinking, Edwards plainly pointed out that the teaching of Scripture is that "the power of his anger is so great that we can't conceive of it." Divine anger "will be intolerable," "exceeding dreadful," and "inconceivably dreadful." Man cannot bear it; nothing will relieve it; time will not lessen it. For eternity, God will pursue the wicked and exact His justice for their sin.

The visitation of wrath on the unrepentant would bring God great glory, Edwards taught. God had no second thoughts about the judgment. He would not struggle or hesitate to carry it out. As Edwards preached in "Torments," He did all things to manifest His glory, including judgment:

> 'TIS GOD'S GLORY that he is a jealous God as well as that he is an infinitely gracious God. When Moses desired to see God's glory and God answered him by proclaiming his glory, they were both in his mercy and grace, and also his jealousy. His name that he proclaimed to Moses consisted of them two things. Exodus 34:6–7, "And the Lord passed by before him, and proclaimed, The Lord, The Lord God, merciful and gracious, long-suffering, abundant in goodness and truth"; and then in the next verse, "That will by no means clear the guilty; visiting the iniquity of the fathers upon the children, and upon the children's children, unto the third and to the fourth generation." 'Tis God's glory that he is a consuming fire, and he has appointed the damnation of the wicked on purpose to show forth this glory of his. As the Scripture expressly teaches us, Romans 9:22, "What if God, willing to show his wrath, and to make his power known, endured with much long-suffering the vessels of wrath fitted to destruction." (*Works* 14, 307)

In reading such texts, modern readers often wonder about their justice and fairness. A deep and justifiable sadness for the lost washes over us as we read of their eternal destruction.

Edwards undoubtedly felt the same way, but his theocentric perspective left his questions tethered to his trust of the Lord. Edwards knew from Scripture that God does all things for His glory. His personal judgment, carried out as a result of His personal wrath, results in His personal glory. The Scripture was clear on this matter.

With this backdrop in place, Edwards next covered the character of sin. In a world where we are trained to explain away sin, Edwards put it into proper perspective in "Torments":

> [R]EBELLION AGAINST GOD'S authority and contempt of his majesty, which every sin contains, is an infinite evil, because it has that infinite aggravation of being against an infinitely excellent and glorious majesty and most absolute authority. A sin against a more excellent being is doubtless greater than against a less excellent; and therefore, sins against one infinite in majesty, authority and excellency must be infinite in aggravation, and so deserves not a finite, but an infinite punishment, which can be only by its being infinite in duration. And then one sin deserves that the punishment should be to that degree of intenseness as to be the destruction of the creature, because every sin is an act of hostility, and 'tis fit that God's enemies should be destroyed.

The lives of unrepentant sinners heap up just condemnation from a holy and gracious God:

IF EVERY SIN, therefore, though comparatively small, deserves eternal death and destruction, how dreadful then is the deserved punishment of wicked men, whose hearts are full of sin, full of inveterate implacable enmity to God and all that is good, and set upon all manner of evil: whose very natures are full of sin as a viper is full of poison, and who have lived all their days in sinful practices; who have committed sin continually, as constantly as they have rose or lay down, or eat or drank, yea, from whom sin has flowed as continually as water from a spring; who have every day been practicing of known sins; that have disobeyed God to his face time after time incessantly; have every day cast contempt upon God's power, upon his justice and holiness, and affronted his majesty and slighted his mercy; have stopped their ears to commands, to calls and warnings, and instead of growing better, have grown worse and worse the more God commands and calls; who have committed many great sins, have grossly transgressed God's holy law. (*Works* 14, 309–10)

If Edwards showed in his preaching that God's wrath is personal, he also showed that sin on the part of humanity is personal. Sin is an offense committed against God. It is entirely natural; people do it without thinking, even as they do it as the result of sustained planning. As a transgression against God and His holy character, sin calls for God's judgment.

Edwards next offered a number of vivid descriptions of the judgment. First he considered Mark 9:44, zeroing in on the phrase "Where their worm dieth not":

ANOTHER METAPHOR THAT IS used to express this tor-ment, is the worm that never dies. Mark 9:44, "Where their worm dieth not." It is taken from Isaiah 66:24, "And they shall go forth, and look upon the carcasses of the men that have transgressed against me: for their worm shall not die, [neither shall their fire be quenched]." The expression of the worm's not dying in the carcasses of these men alludes to this: when a dead carcass lies upon the face of the earth till it begins to putrefy, it will presently be overrun with worms; the carcass will be filled within and without with worms gnawing upon it. And the expression of their fire's not being quenched alludes to the custom of the heathens, when any of them died, to burn them in a fire and so en-tomb their ashes. Now the Prophet says, "Their worm shall not die." When a dead carcass lies putrefying upon the earth, after a while the carcass will be consumed and the worms will die, but the worms that shall gnaw upon the carcasses of these men shall not; that is, their souls shall always be tormented. The similitude holds forth exceeding misery: how miserable must a man be, to be alive and yet have his flesh and bowels and vitals all filled with worms continually gnawing upon his body, as they do upon a dead carcass. (*Works* 14, 310–11)

Next he looked at the fiery destruction of Sodom (Genesis 19:1–29) and how it might parallel hellfire:

NOW WHEN THE DESTRUCTION of Sodom is said to be by the raining of brimstone and fire out of heaven, it seems to have been by miraculous thunder and lightning. The fire of lightning is brimstone and fire, or the burning of a sulfurous matter. It is probable, therefore, that they were destroyed by thick and perpetual flashes of lightning and claps of thunder. 'Tis a way of dying that nature has a peculiar horror of. And what a dreadful picture does it give us of the destruction of hell, that it shall be like perpetual flashes of lightning with amazing claps of thunder upon the heads of the wicked, piercing their souls through and through. Is hell as Sodom was, all full of nothing but fire and brimstone, continual incessant peals of thunder and glaring flashes of lightning upon everyone's head, in everyone's face and through everyone's heart, and that without any cessation, which they shall feel to the utmost and yet live to feel more? It shall not be as when anyone is killed with lightning in this world: he is killed in a moment and neither hears, nor perhaps feels, anything, or if he does, 'tis but for a moment. But in hell, they shall feel it all; they shall feel the dismal pain and rendings of soul that it will cause, and that without ceasing. It will not be one flash of light-ning, and then an intermission, and another by and by, but the lightning will be one perpetual glare, and all in the same soul. (*Works* 14, 317)

In each of these descriptions of hell Edwards showed how the calamities of ancient Sodom offer only a dim foreshad-owing of the horrors of hell. On earth, human carcasses are lifeless, but in hell the wicked would feel the "worms con-tinually gnawing upon his body." In Sodom, the wicked were felled in an instant; in hell, "the lightning will be one per-petual glare." As bad as earthly death and judgment proved to be, they were mercifully temporal in a way that hellish judg-ment would not be.

Unsettling Images from the Realm of Destruction

Edwards offered the most horrifying depictions of hell in his sermon "Sinners in the Hands of an Angry God," a homily on Deuteronomy 32:35 (KJV), "Their foot shall slide in due time." The sermon is the most famous in American history. It is starkly terrifying, filled with apocalyptic imagery that bears looking into. First, Edwards compared God's vengeance to mighty rivers:

THE WRATH OF GOD is like great waters that are dammed for the present; they increase more and more, and rise higher and higher, till an outlet is given, and the longer the stream is stopped, the more rapid and mighty is its course, when once it is let loose. 'Tis true, that judgment against your evil works has not been executed hitherto; the floods of God's vengeance have been withheld; but your guilt in the meantime is constantly increasing, and you are every day treasuring up more wrath; the waters are continually rising and waxing more and more mighty; and there is nothing but the mere pleasure of God that holds the waters back that are unwilling to be stopped, and press hard to go forward; if God should only withdraw his hand from the floodgate, it would immediately fly open, and the fiery floods of the fierceness and wrath of God would rush forth with inconceivable fury, and would come upon you with omnipotent power; and if your strength were ten thousand times greater than it is, yea, ten thousand times greater than the strength of the stoutest, sturdiest devil in hell, it would be nothing to withstand or endure it. (*Works* 22, 410–11)

He then pictured God as a bowman with a bead on His target (Psalm 11:2):

THE BOW OF GOD'S WRATH is bent, and the arrow made ready on the string, and Justice bends the arrow at your heart, and strains the bow, and it is nothing but the mere pleasure of God, and that of an angry God, without any promise or obligation at all, that keeps the arrow one moment from being made drunk with your blood. (*Works* 22, 411)

In the sermon's abiding image, Edwards compared the sinner to a spider held back from an open flame by the "mere pleasure" of the Lord:

THE GOD THAT HOLDS you over the pit of hell, much as one holds a spider, or some loathsome insect, over the fire, abhors you, and is dreadfully provoked; his wrath towards you burns like fire; he looks upon you as worthy of nothing else, but to be cast into the fire; he is of purer eyes than to bear to have you in his sight; you are ten thousand times so abominable in his eyes as the most hateful venomous serpent is in ours. You have offended him infinitely more than ever a stubborn rebel did his prince: and yet 'tis nothing but his hand that holds you from falling into the fire every moment; 'tis to be ascribed to nothing else, that you did not go to hell the last night; that you was suffered to awake again in this world, after you closed your eyes to sleep: and there is no other reason to be given why you have not dropped into hell since you arose in the morning, but that God's hand has held you up; there is no other

reason to be given why you han't gone to hell since you
have sat here in the house of God, provoking his pure eyes
by your sinful wicked manner of attending his solemn worship: yea, there is nothing else that is to be given as a
reason why you don't this very moment drop down into
hell. (*Works* 22, 411–12)

In a particularly visceral passage based on Isaiah 63:3, he pictured the Lord as the trampler of the wicked in a winepress:

HOW AWFUL ARE THOSE WORDS, Isaiah 63:3, which are
the words of the great God, "I will tread them in mine
anger, and will trample them in my fury, and their blood
shall be sprinkled upon my garments, and I will stain all
my raiment." 'Tis perhaps impossible to conceive of words
that carry in them greater manifestations of these three
things, viz. contempt, and hatred, and fierceness of indig-
nation. If you cry to God to pity you, he will be so far from
pitying you in your doleful case, or showing you the least
regard or favor, that instead of that he'll only tread you
under foot: and though he will know that you can't bear
the weight of omnipotence treading upon you, yet he won't
regard that, but he will crush you under his feet without
mercy; he'll crush out your blood, and make it fly, and it
shall be sprinkled on his garments, so as to stain all his raiment. He will not only hate you, but he will have you in the

utmost contempt; no place shall be thought fit for you, but under his feet, to be trodden down as the mire of the streets. (*Works* 22, 414)

The collective weight of these images boggles the mind. In our age, when many professing Christians question the doctrine of hell, warm to the unbiblical idea of universal salvation, and reenvision certain texts along annihilationist lines, Edwards's remarkable images lead us back to the plain and dreadful teaching of certain Scripture passages.

The various pictures Edwards paints of hell—as a flood of vengeance, an arrow aimed at the heart, a great furnace over which sinners dangle, and a winepress filled with blood—each draw out an aspect of hell. The Scripture looks at the realm from various angles, all of which contribute to a general conception of it as a place of the most intense suffering. Those of us who have accepted an unbalanced view of God—where God is only loving and gentle and has no place in His character for just wrath—will struggle with these images. We will be tempted to omit or at the very least ignore this aspect of His character.

Though we tremble at the scriptural testimony on judgment, we must take care that we do not allow our emotions, however moved by the fate of the lost, to overwhelm the plain teaching of the Bible. As Edwards brings out in a number of sermons, including those covered above, the Scripture presents God's judgment of the wicked as an outworking of His majesty. In a way that is hard for us to comprehend, the fury of God's justice brings glory to God. His justice proceeds from His righteousness, His holy hatred of sin. The existence of unholiness calls into necessity His judgment.

Edwards's own mind boggled at these realities. Yet he knew that the Scripture spoke with piercing clarity about the day of judgment and hell. Even if he did not fully know the mind of God, he knew that the Lord was trustworthy and right. If God was God, then by definition He was holy and just, however much the finite mind might grapple with His decrees. He expressed this belief in his sermon "The Justice of God in the Damnation of Sinners," based on Romans 3:19:

> 'TIS MEET THAT GOD should order all these things, according to his own pleasure. By reason of his greatness and glory, by which he is infinitely above all, he is worthy to be sovereign, and that his pleasure should in all things take place: he is worthy that he should make himself his end, and that he should make nothing but his own wisdom his rule in pursuing that end, without asking leave or counsel of any, and without giving account of any of his matters. 'Tis fit that he that is absolutely perfect, and infinitely wise, and the fountain of all wisdom, should determine everything by his own will, even things of the greatest importance, such as the eternal salvation or damnation of sinners. 'Tis meet that he should be thus sovereign, because he is the first being, the eternal being, whence all other beings

are. He is the creator of all things; and all are absolutely and universally dependent on him; and therefore 'tis meet that he should act as the sovereign possessor of heaven and earth. (*Works* 19, 347–48)

As Edwards teaches, the Lord is "absolutely perfect" and "infinitely wise." We are not. We have no right to question God, to make Him bow before us and answer to us. Our response to His holy Word and the wisdom it reveals is obedience and trust. He is the "sovereign possessor" of all; we are but the possessed.

As Edwards's example instructs us, we are called by Him to shirk the foolishness of this world and embrace the truth of Scripture and its doctrines, including the unpopular doctrines of hell and judgment. We are called by Him to preach the truth, including the unfashionable truth regarding damnation and torment. We are called by Him to set the matter in theocentric terms, to show how God is right, that sin is an offense against God, and God is just to punish it. We are called by Him to preach the full scriptural counsel about hell, referencing and explaining the vivid pictures of that realm the Bible provides. We are not called to reshape the faith to make it more palatable to the sinful heart. God requires us to be faithful to His Word and, like Edwards so powerfully did, to preach the whole counsel, including the parts that unsettle us and cause us to pray for mercy for those far off from the Lord.

The Certainty of God's Judgment

It is not easy to work one's way through the doctrine of punishment. Yet as Edwards showed, judgment is an important, if secondary, aspect of the ultimate plan of God and the mission of Christ. The second coming in particular will reveal the awesome majesty of the Savior. Sinners who derided Him, denied Him, ignored Him, took Him for granted, hated Him, mocked Him, made Him a joke, used Him as a curse word, reshaped Him in their image, and failed to take His Word seriously will meet a terrible end. To cite the ominous words of the prophet Hosea, those who have sowed to the wind "shall reap the whirlwind" (Hosea 8:7).

More terrible than any mythic journey to Mordor or any other realm, the scriptural testimony on hell commands our sober attention and assent. It implores us to share the gospel with all we can while we still have time. It drives us to pray for the lost so that they may escape the judgment of the Lord. It reminds us of what we have been spared, knowledge that cannot help but bring us to our knees in thanksgiving to God for the atonement of His Son. The biblical doctrine of hell reshapes all our thinking about the future of this world and its inhabitants. Soon, we know, the righteous justice of Christ will sweep over the earth. Soon the visions of Scripture elaborated by Edwards and others will come true. In that day, none will resist the Lord.

Preparing for Eternity

Acknowledge the Reality of Hell

The first lesson we can learn from Jonathan Edwards on the subject of hell is quite simple. Like him, we need to believe in eternal punishment. The Bible, especially the New Testament, makes abundantly clear that hell is real, an actual place, and the eternal destination of much of the human race (Matthew 7:14). Scripture speaks much of hell, with Jesus raising the subject more than any other biblical voice (for starters, see Matthew 5:22, 29–30; 18:8–9; 25:46; Mark 9:43–48; Luke 16:23; John 3:36; 5:24; 10:28).

It is important that we modern people recognize the difficulty we naturally have with accepting the reality of hell. We will be tempted by our modern sensibilities to refashion the doctrine, tweak it, apologize for it, dislike it, and reject it. Many of us have accepted tenets of thought that make accepting the whole counsel of Christian doctrine a challenging proposition. Our godless age tempts us to sift biblical truth for the parts we like, instead of allowing God to speak authoritatively into our lives.

We are responsible for declaring the gospel, not for telling people what they want to hear. As is quite clear from American history, preaching a feel-good, personally enhancing message of positive religious thinking can attract quite a crowd. It's not difficult in this country to win a large following with a religious message. It is far more challenging to build a church through faithful preaching of the biblical gospel—the message of redemption from judgment through the atoning death and life-giving resurrection of Christ. If we only aspire to build a nice building, win some hearers, raise some money, and do some positive things, we can tailor our message as we see fit—the specific content will follow the spirit of the times. But if we would see sinners won from hell, lives dramatically changed by the Word, and disciples of Christ raised up, then like Edwards we will need to embrace the gospel, preach the whole counsel of the Word, and seek to make true disciples for the glory of God Almighty.

The more we believe in hell and allow it its rightful place in our theology, the more seriously we will take our Christianity. We will take God for granted less and live in gratitude more. We will praise Him with wide-eyed gratitude for the deliverance He has wrought in our lives. We will live more seriously for His glory, remembering that our salvation has come at a great price and accomplished an incredible end. We will approach the basic duties of our lives with heightened awareness of the opportunities before us to glorify our great Savior. In these and many other ways, living with our deliverance from hell in full view will change us.

Preach Hell

*M*any people read the culture today and conclude, rightly, that preaching hell will turn hearers off. So they emphasize the positive aspects of Christianity and tuck their belief in hell away. While no one would urge believers to preach only judgment to the world, the biblical figures who have gone before us preached a bold message of salvation from judgment (see Acts 2 and 4, for example). It makes little sense, after all, to preach only salvation. Salvation from what, we might ask? From oneself? From psychological problems? From sadness? Well, yes, to all of the above and more. But far more importantly, we need to preach salvation from judgment, specifically, from the day of judgment and the eternal punishment in hell that will follow. In addition, our efforts to massage the message may have little effect and, surprisingly, even impair our attempts to reach the lost. We preach hell not because of its evangelistic results, of course, but out of a desire to remain faithful to the scriptural gospel. With that said, hell is a potent reality, as Edwards recognized. It has led many to flee to the arms of Christ for salvation. The preaching of Christ, of the apostles, and of countless figures throughout church history testify to the fact that sinners often repent as a result of hearing both the bad news, future condemnation for sin, and the good news, the glorious atonement of Christ. Too many Christians today speak ill of "hellfire and brimstone" preaching. We need to tell the truth about hell with balance and humility; but just as biblical figures did not shy away from preaching God's just punishment of sin, neither should we.

We can take great encouragement from figures like Edwards who preached heaven and hell alike with great passion and feeling. Our presentation of hell should, like his, stir the heart and trouble the conscience. The images of hell in the Bible are not meant to soothe, after all. They are meant to unsettle, to drive the lost to take their sin seriously and cry out to God for mercy. This is what Edwards sought in his day; this is what we must seek in ours.

CHAPTER THREE

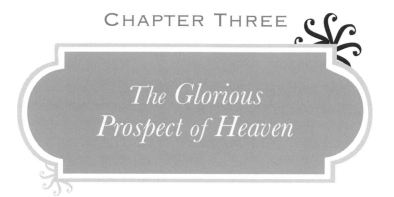

The Glorious Prospect of Heaven

*C*hristians are called in the New Testament "strangers and pilgrims," a striking metaphor for the Christian life (1 Peter 2:11). On this earth, believers are not "residents." They are likened to an alien race, a nomadic tribe making its way through a wilderness. There is an element of sadness in this description, a note of yearning. Christians have no true home in this place. Our home is another realm: heaven.

While we travel, every Christian sees a bit of heaven, finds its light drawing them closer. Yet few of us have recognized the full glory of the life to come. In our subject, Jonathan Edwards, we have located an excellent guide of the realm to come. Edwards's writings, written long ago, teach us that heaven is real. It is a grand spectacle, the greatest of any we can imagine. As the Scripture teaches, it is the realm of glory, the very substance of all our hope (John 14, 2 Corinthians 5, Hebrews 11, Revelation 21–22). It is not small and weak and relatively unimportant, as we so often render it. It is great, and real, and *coming*.

In this chapter, we examine Edwards's vision of heaven. We look at the following sermons: "True Saints, When Absent from the Body, Are Present with the Lord," which shows us that heaven is real; "Nothing Upon Earth Can Represent the Glories of Heaven," "The Pure in Heart Blessed," and "The Many Mansions," all of which show various degrees of our heavenly joy; "Serving God in Heaven," which teaches that we will serve the Lord in heaven; "Degrees of Glory," which reveals that our earthly lives resound in eternity; and "Heaven Is a World of Love," the grandest sermon of them all. We will not necessarily construct a rigorous argument in this chapter, but rather present various depictions of heaven from Edwards's material that will reinvigorate us for the journey ahead. In the pastor's awe-inspiring preaching and teaching on heaven, we find fresh faith and courage to journey on through barren wilderness in search of a place of perfect peace and joy.

Heaven Is Real

To understand the Edwardsean conception of heaven, we need to know first of all that the pastor believed that heaven was real. This may sound obvious, but Edwards knew that many Christians struggled to keep this belief in sight. In a sermon now called "True Saints, When Absent from the Body, Are Present with the Lord," based on 2 Corinthians 5:8, Edwards sought to pull his hearers away from their temporal concerns to show them that they would soon rest with the Lord. Death could come for them in an instant, but they did not need to fear it if they trusted in Christ. Heaven awaited:

> WHEN WE ARE ABSENT from our dear friends, they are out of sight; but when we are with them, we have the opportunity and satisfaction of seeing them. So while the saints are in the body, and are absent from the Lord, he is in several respects out of sight; 1 Peter 1:8, "Whom having not seen, ye love: in whom, though now ye see him not, yet believing," etc. They have indeed, in this world, a spiritual sight of Christ; but they see through a glass darkly, and with great interruption: but in heaven, they see him face to face (1 Corinthians 13:12). "The pure in heart are blessed; for they shall see God" (Matthew 5:8). (*Works* 25, 229)

Heaven allowed glorified believers the opportunity to behold their Lord. Edwards helps us to see that heaven, fundamentally, is about fellowship with God. Heaven is the realm of God that contains "all the glory of the Godhead." No matter what unanswered questions we may have—Will we know one another? What will we look like? What will we do?—we may know for certain that the focus of heaven is our God. It is not our desires and whims that will direct things in heaven, but His. However we might imagine the shape of our life to come, we may rest assured that the Lord will order all things perfectly.

In heaven, we will think much about our redemption, Edwards suggested. Contemplation of God's plan of salvation will produce more love for the Lord than we can imagine:

> AND WHEN THE SOULS of the saints leave their bodies, to go to be with Christ, they behold the marvelous glory of that great work of his, the work of redemption, and of the glorious way of salvation by him; which the angels desire to look into. They have a most clear view of the unfath-omable depths of the manifold wisdom and knowledge of God; and the most bright displays of the infinite purity and holiness of God, that do appear in that way and work: and see in another manner, than the saints do here, what is the breadth and length and depth and height of the grace and love of Christ, appearing in his redemption. And as they see the unspeakable riches and glory of the attribute of God's grace, so they most clearly behold and understand Christ's eternal and unmeasurable dying love to them in particular. And in short they see everything in Christ that tends to kindle and enflame love, and everything that tends to gratify love, and everything that tends to satisfy them: and that in the most clear and glorious manner, without

any darkness or delusion, without any impediment or interruption. (*Works* 25, 230)

Though they faced different challenges than we do, Edwards's people experienced the same struggle to embrace heaven that many of us do. They loved their earthly lives. They feared death, wondering occasionally if the promise of heaven would come true. They grieved deeply at the funerals of Christians, sometimes feeling more sadness than joy. Edwards ministered to people who struggled with such issues by reassuring them of the certain home of the Christian. "[W]hen the souls of the saints leave their bodies," he reminded them, they "go to be with Christ" in heaven. There they "do see him as he is." Death signals no lasting tragedy for the believer. One moment we are in our bodies, navigating the complexities of this realm. The next, we are ushered into the presence of Christ.

Upon meeting Christ, Edwards went on, we recognize and worship Him as our "glorious and loving Redeemer." The fact of Christ's substitutionary atonement does not fade into the distance for us in heaven. It grows more beautiful. As the "sun" rises in the morning and brings illumination, so will our ascension to heaven cause the glory of Christ's death and resurrection to shine afresh.

This kind of heavenly happiness will not fade away as it does on earth. Later in "True Saints," Edwards noted that Christians in heaven are "a thousand times" happier than we are because of their intimate association with Jesus:

ON THESE ACCOUNTS the saints in heaven must needs be under a thousand times greater advantage than we here, for a full view of the state of the church on earth, and a speedy, direct and certain acquaintance with all its affairs, in every part. And that which gives them much greater advantage for such an acquaintance, than the things already mentioned, is their being constantly in the immediate presence of Christ, and in the enjoyment of the most perfect intercourse with him, who is the King who manages all these affairs, and has an absolutely perfect knowledge of them. Christ is the head of the whole glorified assembly; they are mystically his glorified body: and what the head sees, it sees for the information of the whole body, according to its capacity; and what the head enjoys, is for the joy of the whole body. (*Works* 25, 237)

In heaven, Jesus is the lodestar. He is the center, the substance, the focus, and His joy is the "joy of the whole body." None will find their happiness diminished in the world to come; all will have perfect delight in His presence. Insights like this from Edwards are worth pondering and soaking up.

Heaven Is a Glorious City

Some of what makes heaven hard to believe in is that we have not seen it and thus have little sense of what it looks like.

In his sermon "Nothing Upon Earth Can Represent the Glories of Heaven," derived from Revelation 21:18, Edwards reminds us that heaven is a city, albeit unlike any we have ever seen:

> HEAVEN IS LIKENED in Scripture to a splendid and glorious city. Many men are ever surprised and amazed by the sight of a splendid city. We need not to be told how often heaven is called the holy city of God. Other cities are built by men, but this city, we are told, was built immediately by God himself. His hands reared up the stately mansions of this city, and his wisdom contrived them. Hebrews 11:10, "For he looked for a city which has foundations, whose builder and maker is God." Other cities that are royal cities, that is, the cities that are the seats of kings and where they keep their courts, are commonly, above all others, stately and beautiful; but heaven, we are told, is the royal city of God, where the King of heaven and earth dwells, and displays his glory. Hebrews 12:22, "The city of the living God." (*Works* 14, 141)

In this city, the realm of perfection, mankind would revel in the greatness of God. Edwards explained this in his sermon, "The Pure in Heart Blessed," based on Matthew 5:8. The Lord had expressly made the heart of man for heaven by fitting it to become perfectly happy:

WHEN GOD GAVE MAN his capacity of happiness, he
doubtless made provision for the filling of it. There was
some good that God had in his eye when he made the
vessel, and made it of such dimensions, that he knew to be
sufficient to fill it and to contain which the vessel was prepared; and doubtless that, whatever it be, is man's true
blessedness. And that good which is found not to be commensurate to men's capacity and natural cravings, and
never can equal it, it certainly denotes it not to be that
wherein men's happiness consists.

Your heart is not made for this earth, Edwards told his hearers. It was made for another realm. Happiness here is fleeting
and insufficient. Happiness in heaven is full and undimmed,
never ceasing, always supplied by the love of God:

BUT THE FOUNTAIN that supplies that joy and delight
which the soul has in seeing God is sufficient to fill the vessel,
because it is infinite. He that sees the glory of God, he in his
measure beholds that that there is no end of. The understanding may extend itself as far [as] it will; it doth but take
its flight out into an endless expanse and dive into a bottomless ocean. It may discover more and more of the beauty
and loveliness of God, but it never will exhaust the fountain.
Man may as well swallow up the ocean as he can extend his
faculties to the utmost of God's excellency. (*Works* 17, 72)

As is clear in this quotation, Edwards believed that happiness, like knowledge, would be progressive in heaven, ever increasing. Yet, this did not lessen the happiness that the glorified believer would experience. All who went to heaven would experience "full satisfaction":

> HOW BLESSED THEREFORE are they that do see God, that are come to this exhaustless fountain! They have obtained that delight that gives full satisfaction; being come to this pleasure, they neither do nor can desire any more. They can sit down fully contented, and take up with this enjoyment forever and ever, and desire no change. After they have had the pleasures of beholding the face of God millions of ages, it won't grow a dull story; the relish of this delight will be as exquisite as ever. There is enough still for the utmost employment of every faculty. (*Works* 17, 73)

We often make the pleasures of this world our standard for happiness. Yet even the best and most lasting joys of this world cannot fractionally compare to the goodness of heaven. Living in heaven, Edwards tells us, is like taking "flight out into an endless expanse" and plunging "into a bottomless ocean" of the "beauty and loveliness of God."

None of this will prove "a dull story," as our earthly joys often do. God has made lasting delight in earthly experiences and possessions evasive. We lose happiness easily here. We grow bored with our favorite things. We easily sense something of the ennui of this world, the listlessness, the tendency to break down and stagnate. We will not know such a deadening pattern in heaven. Our enhanced senses will handle as much delight as they possibly can for all of eternity. We will know joy upon joy, delight upon delight, "forever and ever."

Mansions for All

The gold standard of earthly achievement has been, for centuries, a mansion. Though we might initially chastise such a desire, it seems from the Bible that we were made to desire a heavenly mansion, a place where we can rest in satisfaction and ease, as John 14:2 promises. Edwards elaborated on this text in his sermon "Many Mansions":

> LET ALL BE HENCE EXHORTED, earnestly to seek that they may be admitted to a mansion in heaven. You have heard that this is God's house: it is his temple. If David, when he was in the wilderness of Judah, and in the land of Jeshua, and of the Philistines, so longed that he might again return into the land of Israel, that he might have a place in the house of God here on earth, and prized a place there so much, though it was but that of a doorkeeper; then how great in happiness will it be to have a place in this heavenly temple of God. If they are looked upon as enjoying an high privilege that have a seat appointed there in kings' courts, or an apartment in kings' palaces, especially those

that have an abode there in the quality of the king's children; then how great a privilege will it be to have an apartment or mansion assigned us in God's heavenly palace, and
to have a place there as his children. How great is their
glory and honor that are admitted to be of the household
of God. (*Works* 19, 743)

Edwards's words show that God intends for His people to live
satisfied, restful, enjoyable lives in heaven. This is what the
mansion signifies—not self-glorifying wealth, but the abundant, generous gift of God to His people. On this earth Christians know suffering, poverty, and want to varying degrees. It
is a sure hope that in the life to come, the Lord will give us an
endless bounty of goodness and a "high privilege" that has
never been known on this earth (1 Corinthians 2:6–10).

We will not hole up in our heavenly mansions, however.
In the world to come, we will gather as the family of God:

HEAVEN IS THE HOUSE where God dwells with his family
God is represented in Scripture as having a family; and
though some of this family are now on earth, yet in so
being, they are abroad, or not at home, but all going home.
Ephesians 3:15, "Of whom the whole family in heaven and
earth is named." Heaven is the place that God has built for
himself and his children. God has many children, and the
place designed for 'em is heaven. And therefore the saints,
being the children of God, are said to be of the household

of God. Ephesians 2:19, "Now therefore ye are no more strangers and foreigners, but fellow citizens with the saints, and of the household of God." God is represented as an householder, or the head of a family, and heaven is his house. (*Works* 19, 738)

In heaven, we will dwell together with God. We will gather as a joyful family to celebrate the One who has called us to Himself. We will experience perfect communion and intimate fellowship with one another and with our God. We will make our way to our mansion and take unforeseen delight in the home prepared for us.

Serving God in Heaven

Just because heaven is a place of worship does not mean that it is a tame, lazy, boring realm. According to Edwards's sermon "Serving God in Heaven," a meditation on Revelation 22:3, the ideal realm would feature mankind in his ideal state. This meant action, not passivity:

BUT MAN'S POWERS of action were given him for action. God aimed at action, in giving man such capacities of action. And therefore when the reasonable creature is in action, or in the exercise of those powers of action which God hath given it, then 'tis in its more perfect state if its acts are suitable to the rational nature, and consequently is more happy than in a state of idleness. (*Works* 17, 254)

In serving the Lord, man was fulfilling the design-plan God had created for him:

> THEREFORE, WHEN MAN serves God, he acts most accord-
> ing to his nature. He is employed in that sort of action that
> is most distinguishing of him from the beasts. He acts then
> in a way most according to the end of his formation, and
> most agreeable to his make and formation of the human
> nature itself. A man never acts so rationally as when he
> serves God. No actions [are] so agreeable to reason, and all
> that are contrary to God's service are contrary to reason.
> And therefore, doubtless, his happiness consists in serving
> God. (*Works* 17, 255)

This illuminates why we naturally gravitate to work. Even without the light of revelation, there is something in the heart of a person that relishes productivity. Most of us are happiest when put to good ends. The satisfaction we enjoy in such work foreshadows our lives in the age to come, which will be filled with all kinds of fruitful endeavors in the name of our Lord. Edwards spelled this out further in "Serving God":

> THE SAINTS IN HEAVEN will take great delight in serving
> of [God], as they delight in doing that which is just and
> right. Justice is what they delight in; if anything is right and
> equal, it is sufficient to make those spirits that are made
> perfect to love it and take pleasure [in] it. They will see

those charms in equity that will cause them to have a perfect love to it. Saints' love to equity and justice in this world
is not perfect. Sometimes a love to other things prevails
over it. A saint here may be drawn to do those things that
are contrary to it, but it will not be so in heaven, where the
soul shall be brought to its perfect rectitude of nature.

He continued:

> THEY WILL BE SENSIBLE that 'tis most reasonable that God
> should be their ruler, in that he has redeemed them. They
> will see that all the service which they can render to him is
> but a small recompense for that great redemption. They
> will be sensible then how great the redemption was, much
> more sensible than they are now; for then, they will be sen-
> sible how terrible the destruction is that they were
> redeemed from, and shall know by experience how glori-
> ous the happiness which was purchased for them. (*Works*
> 17, 256)

As Edwards showed, the reality of redemption will not sit
lightly on the minds of the glorified saints. It will drive us to
serve the Lord with fullness of joy. Heaven is a place of service, but not rote service of the kind we all know well on earth.
We will work for the Lord with the happiest of hearts.

Degrees of Glory in the Afterlife

Edwards believed that our earthly lives counted in the afterlife. In his sermon "Degrees of Glory," based on 2 Corinthians 9:6, he argued that the believer who pursues the glory of God in this life will experience greater honor than a lax believer. The pastor set forth this view early in the sermon:

THE SCRIPTURES DECLARE that God will hereafter reward every man according to his works; as Matthew 16:27, "For the Son of man shall come in the glory of his Father with his angels; and then he shall reward every man according to his works"; and in many other places. Now, by this we but justly understand only that Christ rewards everyone according to the quantity of his works, viz. that he will reward good to them that have done good, and evil to them that have done evil; but also that the reward will be in proportion to men's works. Thus it shall be with the wicked: their punishment will be in proportion to their wicked works; as is abundantly manifest. Thus we read, it shall be more tolerable for some of them than others at the day of judgment. And Christ signifies the different degrees of punishment in hell by the different degrees of capital punishments among the Jews, in Matthew 5:22. "Whosoever shall be angry with his brother without a cause shall be in danger of the judgment." And as wicked men shall in

this sense be rewarded according to their works, viz. in proportion, so doubtless will the godly. Yea, the rewards being
according to our works, our labor is expressly in this sense
applied to the godly by the Apostle. 1 Corinthians 3:8, "Now
he that planteth and he that watereth are one: and every
man shall receive his own reward according to his own
labor." (*Works* 19, 616)

Though we might instinctively think that every Christian will
occupy the same position in heaven, Edwards argued that it
was not so. He grounded his argument in Scripture:

GOD HAS ABUNDANTLY promised to reward the good
works of the saints in another world. Christ has said that if
we do but give a cup [of cold water only, we shall in no
wise lose our reward]. But how can this be, if it be so that
whether they do more good works or fewer, all that have
just the same reward? When a person has a good work
before him to be done, how can he say with himself to
encourage himself to do, "If I do it, I shall be rewarded for
it; I shall in no case lose my reward"; if at the same time it
be true that he shall have as great a reward, if he lets it
alone as if he does it; and he shall have as much future
happiness, if he does few good works as many? There can
be no such thing as any reward at all for good works,

unless they are rewarded with some additional degree of happiness. If nothing be added, then there is nothing gained. (*Works* 19, 616–17)

Living with heavenly rewards in mind was not an option, as Edwards found in his study of the Word. It was:

A DUTY EXPRESSLY COMMANDED. Matthew 6:19–20, "Lay not up for yourselves treasures upon earth, where moth and rust doth corrupt, and where thieves break through and steal: but lay up for yourselves treasures in heaven, where neither moth nor rust doth corrupt, and where thieves do not break through nor steal." By laying up treasure in heaven is not only meant obtain some inheritance there, but to be adding to it; as is evident by the comparison made between this and what is forbidden, viz. laying up treasure on earth. By which Christ don't mean that we should get nothing in this world, but not do as worldly-minded men do, be striving insatiably to hoard up, and keep adding to our worldly good things; but rather strive to add to our inheritance in heaven, and heap up treasure there; labor daily to increase our interest there by doing good works, and abounding in them; as appears by [the] Luke 12:33. "Sell that ye have, and give alms; provide yourselves bags which wax not old, a treasure in the heavens." (*Works* 19, 621–22)

Edwards's argument matches the plain teaching of Scripture. The way that we live on this earth affects our heavenly status. The more that we live for the Lord with the little time that we have here, the more He will reward us in the life to come. Day-to-day life, with moment-by-moment, even second-by-second decisions, counts. It is not all a wash, or all the same to God. The thoughts we think, the programs we choose to watch, the evangelistic conversation we try to have, the cup of cold water we give in the name of Christ, the word of correction we offer a straying believer, the prayer we say as we hurry to work—all of this matters to God. All of it impacts, in a way we do not fully understand now, our eternal standing in heaven.

We do not know exactly how things will shake out. It may very well be that the leaders we admire now must take a back seat to saints we have never heard of in heaven. Our earthly calculus for heavenly standing may prove wrong altogether. We do not know, in the end, where the Lord will seat us in His gallery of worship. We do know, however, that the life we live on this earth matters. Every second of our earthly existence counts.

Heaven Is a World of Love

The axis on which heaven turns, according to Edwards in his sermon "Heaven Is a World of Love," is love. In this sermon, one of the pastor's most stirring, his prose spiraled to great heights. The text immediately grabs the reader's attention and permanently affects the way one thinks about heaven. The central idea of "Heaven Is a World of Love" is that God dwells in heaven and fills the realm with the essence of His being, which is love. The text begins on this note:

> HEAVEN IS THE PALACE, or presence-chamber, of the Supreme Being who is both the cause and source of all holy love. God, indeed, with respect to his essence is everywhere. He fills heaven and earth. But yet he is said on some accounts more especially to be in some places rather than others. He was said of old to dwell in the land of Israel above all other lands, and in Jerusalem above all other cities in that land, and in the temple above all other houses in that city, and in the holy of holies above all other apartments in that temple, and on the mercy seat over the ark above all other places in the holy of holies. But heaven is his dwelling place above all other places in the universe. (*Works* 8, 369)

Edwards captures the largeness of God and heaven here. God is gigantic. He is not small or limited. The Lord "fills heaven and earth." Yet heaven "is his dwelling place" in a special way. It is a place where only things that please God may dwell. He will tolerate no sin, no effects of the curse, no beings who do not delight in Him, but only things that are "lovely":

THERE ARE NONE but lovely objects in heaven. There is no odious or polluted person or thing to be seen there. There is nothing wicked and unholy. Revelation 21:27, "And there shall in no wise enter into it anything that defileth, neither whatsoever worketh abomination, or maketh a lie." There is nothing which is deformed either in natural or moral deformity. Everything which is to be beheld there is amiable. The God, who dwells and gloriously manifests himself there, is infinitely lovely. There is to be seen a glorious heavenly Father, a glorious Redeemer; there is to be felt and possessed a glorious Sanctifier. All the persons who belong to that blessed society are lovely. The Father of the family is so, and so are all his children. The Head of the body is so, and so are all the members. Concerning the angels, there are none who are unlovely. There are no evil angels suffered to infest heaven as they do this world. They are not suffered to come near, but are kept at a distance with a great gulf between them. In the church of saints there are no unlovely persons; there are no false professors, none who pretend to be saints, who are persons of an unchristian, hateful spirit and behavior, as is often the case in this world. There is no one object there to give offense, or at any time to give any occasion for any passion or motion of hatred; but every object shall draw forth love. (*Works* 8, 370)

The identifying characteristic of this otherworldly society is love. In the realm of this world, every relationship is tainted by sin in some way. We experience the love of God and mediate it to others, but even among highly mature Christians, affection is not pure. The heavenly society knows no such weaknesses of love. Proceeding from the Godhead and flowing undiminished into all who reside there, love is the fundamental principle, the defining characteristic of existence:

WITH RESPECT TO THE DEGREE of their love, it is perfect. The love which is in the heart of God is perfect, with an absolute, infinite and divine perfection. The love of the angels and saints to God and Christ is perfect in its kind, or with such a perfection as is proper to their nature, perfect with a sinless perfection, and perfect in that it is commensurate with the capacities of their natures. So it is said in the text, when that which is perfect is come, that which is in part shall be done away. Their love shall be without any remains of a contrary principle. Having no pride or selfishness to interrupt or hinder its exercises, their hearts shall be full of love. That which was in the heart as but a grain of mustard seed in this world shall there be as a great tree. The soul which only had a little spark of divine love in it in this world shall be, as it were, wholly turned into love; and be like the sun, not having a spot in it, but being wholly a bright, ardent flame. There shall be no remaining

enmity, distaste, coldness and deadness of heart towards
God and Christ; not the least remainder of any principle of
envy to be exercised towards any angels or saints who are
superior in glory, no contempt or slight towards any who
are inferior. (*Works* 8, 375–76)

More comforting and hopeful words one can scarcely find.
The Northampton pastor compels his hearers to remember
the sweet and sometimes forgotten promises of Scripture. The
"mustard seed" that fights to grow here will surely grow into
"a great tree" in eternity. The soul that fought to taste the love
of God in this earth but battled bitterly against besetting sin,
hurtful situations, and desperate circumstances will find its
"little spark of divine love" turned into "a bright, ardent flame."
Nothing will impair the Christian's love for the Lord, no
"enmity, distaste, coldness and deadness of heart," no "principle of envy," no "contempt or slight." The absence of these
problems so familiar to us who dwell in a sinful world clarify
the wonder and hope of heaven.

It is worth noting that the subject of jealousy occupies a
great deal of space in the sermon. Most believers today avoid
this issue. It's an uncomfortable sin to confront, both in ourselves and others. In a unique way, jealousy poses the power
to altogether destroy love. Where it resides in a heart, it naturally crowds out positive affections. Edwards does not offer
any personal reflection on this matter, but as a highly gifted
person, it is certain that he faced considerable envy in his life.
His words, stemming from personal experience, remind us

that the petty rivalries and bitter envy of this world will have no place in the realm to come:

> THOSE WHO HAVE a lower station in glory than others suffer no diminution of their own happiness by seeing others above them in glory. On the contrary they rejoice in it. All that whole society rejoice in each other's happiness; for the love of benevolence is perfect in them. Everyone has not only a sincere but a perfect good will to every other. Sincere and strong love is greatly gratified and delighted in the prosperity of the beloved. And if the love be perfect, the greater the prosperity of the beloved is, the more is the lover pleased and delighted. For the prosperity of the beloved is, as it were, the food of love; and therefore the greater that prosperity is, the more richly is love feasted. The love of benevolence is delighted in beholding the prosperity of another, as the love of complacence is delighted in viewing the beauty of another. So that the superior prosperity of those who are higher in glory is so far from being any damp to the happiness of saints of lower degree that it is an addition to it, or a part of it. There is undoubtedly an inconceivably pure, sweet and fervent love between the saints in glory; and their love is in proportion to the perfection and amiableness of the objects beloved. And therefore it must necessarily cause delight in them when they

see others' happiness and glory to be in proportion to their amiableness, and so in proportion to their love of them. Those who are highest in glory are those who are highest in holiness, and therefore are those who are most beloved by all the saints. For they love those most who are most holy, and so they will all rejoice in it that they are most happy. And it will be a damp to none of the saints to see them who have higher degrees of holiness and likeness to God to be more loved than themselves; for all shall have as much love as they desire, and as great manifestations of love as they can bear; all shall be fully satisfied. (*Works* 8, 375)

Though the human heart, so prone to competition, struggles with this reality, Edwards taught that heaven would include no jealousy over position or honor earned by holy living. Instead, the joy of one would fuel the joy of all:

AND WHEN THERE IS perfect satisfaction, there is no room for envy. And they will have no temptation to envy those who are above them in glory from their superiors being lifted up with pride. We are apt to conceive that those who are more holy, and more happy than others in heaven, will be elated and lifted up in their spirit above others. Whereas their being above them in holiness implies their being superior to them in humility; for their superior humility is part of their superior holiness. Though all are perfectly free from pride, yet as some will have greater degrees of divine knowledge than others, will have larger capacities to see more of the divine perfections, so they will see more of their own comparative littleness and nothingness, and therefore will be lowest abased in humility. And besides, the inferior in glory will have no temptation to envy those who are higher. For those who are highest will not only be more beloved by the lower saints for their higher holiness, but they will also have more of a spirit of love to others. They will love those who are below them more than other saints of less capacity. They who are in highest degrees of glory will be of largest capacity, and so of greatest knowledge, and will see most of God's loveliness, and consequently will have love to God and love to saints most abounding in their hearts. So that those who are lower in glory will not envy those who are above them. (*Works* 8, 376)

Heaven must be an unearthly place, if this kind of fellowship characterizes it. The love of the saints for one another, a love that flows from the shared affection of the Godhead, so orders their feelings and thoughts that they rejoice fully and completely in the promotion of another. No "What about me?" plagues the minds of children of God in the realm to come. Where they once felt twinges of jealousy mixed in with their genuine happiness for a fellow Christian, in heaven they will know only pure happiness as the Lord honors others for their faithfulness. The blessing of God given to all will serve as the "food of love" that will feed and heighten the happiness of all. Heaven is a world of love, a place where jealousy, narcissism, self-promotion, and bitterness have no place.

Longing for Heaven

All of the preceding promises to awaken our passion for heaven. Considerable trials rise up before us on this earth. Our sin attacks us, and Satan seeks to discourage us from pursuing holiness. The suffering of others can overwhelm us at times and make us feel that our quest is futile. Though we are strangers and pilgrims now, we have great hope. We are redeemed by the Savior. We have seen a vision of a better place where God receives His children. As Edwards described movingly toward the end of "Heaven Is a World of Love," heaven offers all who are faithful to Christ the opportunity to enter "the Paradise of God":

AND ALL THIS in a garden of love, the Paradise of God, where everything has a cast of holy love, and everything conspires to promote and stir up love, and nothing to interrupt its exercises; where everything is fitted by an all-wise God for the enjoyment of love under the greatest advantages. And all this shall be without any fading of the beauty of the objects beloved, or any decaying of love in the lover, and any satiety in the faculty which enjoys love. O! what tranquility may we conclude there is in such a world as this! Who can express the sweetness of this peace? What a calm is this, what a heaven of rest is here to arrive at after persons have gone through a world of storms and tempests, a world of pride, and selfishness, and envy, and malice, and scorn, and contempt, and contention and war? What a Canaan of rest, a land flowing with milk and honey to come to after one has gone through a great and terrible wilderness, full of spiteful and poisonous serpents, where no rest could be found? (*Works* 8, 385)

As we make our way through this life, let us remember: this is what awaits us.

Preparing for Eternity

Believe in Heaven

*T*he main challenge before us is simply this: to believe in heaven. We don't mean any old make-your-own version. We mean the biblical view, one nicely expounded by Edwards in the sermons covered above. Heaven is real. It has a definite character. The book of Revelation in particular teaches us about it. We would do well to study this text to fire our hearts and inform our imaginations about the blessed afterlife. Too often we approach Revelation merely as an apocalyptic puzzle. It certainly is that, but there is also tremendous value in studying heaven to inspire belief in the life to come.

The world around us offers little incentive to adopt the biblical view of heaven. Instead, it encourages us to think about heaven in our own terms, whether as a place where all nice people go, or a realm of ethereal light where one exists in a kind of blessed abstraction, or a place where we meet up with loved ones and favorite pets, or any number of other visions. We must resist these influences. We must listen to the Scripture and the profound teaching of men like Edwards, and we must believe in heaven, and live as if this belief matters.

Comprehend the Multidimensional Nature of Heaven

*E*dwards's material shows us that heaven is not one-sided. There is much to learn and study about it. The Bible offers us numerous pictures of heaven, filling out our conception of the realm, enhancing our anticipation of it. In heaven, we will take up a mansion prepared for us; we will serve the Lord with our talents and abilities; we will rest in the arms of Christ; we will worship the Lord by singing and praising the resurrected Lamb; we will rejoice as faithful Christians receive the acclamation of Almighty God for their lives. This is not all we will do and be in heaven—we possess limited knowledge of the shape of our lives there. We can see clearly, though, that heaven is a realm where we will worship our majestic God in many different ways. If we find ourselves reducing heaven to any one paradigm, we must remind ourselves of the many-sidedness of the blessed life to come. Doing so will stave off unwarranted disinterest and boredom related to heaven and will provoke eagerness and excitement about it. The multidimensional glory of heaven, flowing from the eternal triune God, will soon bring fully into view what we now see "in a mirror dimly" (1 Corinthians 13:12).

CHAPTER FOUR

The Transforming Power of an Eternity-Focused Mind-set

*O*ur last chapter looked at the life of the "stranger and pilgrim," examining what the Christian focuses on as they travel to the world to come. Heaven occupies the mind of the traveler, pushing them on to see their Savior and find their reward. Yet, we might ask, what does this life look like on a daily basis? Are we to live with our heads in the clouds, walking in a daze through our obligations and pastimes? Do we abandon our earthly chores, find a nice hill to sit on, and wait for death?

The biblical figures listed in a passage familiar to many of us, Hebrews 11, offer us a solid answer to our questions. The various heroes listed in this passage all trusted that God would grant them something greater than this world. After celebrating a number of these figures, including Abel, Enoch, Noah, Abraham, and Sarah, the author of the letter tells us that:

> IF THEY HAD BEEN THINKING of that land from which they had gone out, they would have had opportunity to return. But as it is, they desire a better country, that is, a heavenly one. Therefore God is not ashamed to be called their God, for he has prepared for them a city. (Hebrews 11:15–16)

The author later heralds unknown martyrs, men and women now lost to time whose faith made their lives an offering to Christ:

> SOME WERE TORTURED, refusing to accept release, so that they might rise again to a better life. Others suffered mocking and flogging, and even chains and imprisonment. They were stoned, they were sawn in two, they were killed with the sword. They went about in skins of sheep and goats, destitute, afflicted, mistreated—of whom the world was not worthy—wandering about in deserts and mountains, and in dens and caves of the earth. (Hebrews 11:35–38)

Though these heroes did not know all that we do about heaven, they viewed their earthly experiences through the promise of a blessed afterlife. Their belief in the life to come did not result in a Zen-like, otherworldly mental state that enabled them to shut their eyes to sin and sorrow. Rather, the eschatological (future-oriented), heaven-focused mind-set of these heroes formed them into agents of grace, people followed the call of the Lord through the valley of the shadow of death.

Our era presents the eschatological Christian with unique challenges, a number of which we will briefly identify as we piece together what a heavenly minded Christian life looks like today. In this brief closing chapter, we will offer several suggestions to help us adopt an eschatological mindset in our day. We will blend scriptural analysis, Edwardsean teaching, and contemporary perspective to accomplish this goal. We will look at several ways that heaven-focused thinking affects who we are and how we live, including our identity, family, church, work, and witness.

Developing Identity

Jonathan Edwards, like the heroes of the Bible, lived life differently than his peers. He had heaven on the brain. As described in previous books in this series, he took frequent trips to the countryside, mulling over the promise of heaven as he rode his horse through brisk breezes and rolling hills. He thought deeply about this earth, but he considered himself a citizen of another land. Edwards's meditation produced not only deep preaching, but a radically different way of life.

His insights, based on the Bible, can do the same for us. At our core, we can reconceive our existences, rooting them in heaven more than earth. What does this mean, practically? It means that we study Scripture, saturate our minds with it, and learn to think in scriptural categories. We need to commit ourselves to putting the Scripture and its teaching on the afterlife constantly before us so that the Holy Spirit can transform our lives. As we read texts on heaven and hell, meditating deeply on them, we will naturally find that we think of heaven as our true home.

This kind of commitment will influence our lives in numerous ways. We will see ourselves as heaven-bound Christians first, not employees, not parents, not politically concerned citizens, not sports fans. Recognizing ourselves as children of God bound for heaven will prevent us from investing ourselves too deeply in earthly matters. We need this kind of grounding. Church history shows us that Christians are always at risk of losing a biblically balanced lifestyle. For example, we can rightly act on a concern for social justice and compassion, but lose our heart for the gospel in the process, as happened to some professing believers in the early twentieth century. Or, we can overemphasize our citizenship in heaven, and effectively pull out of this world, as some Christians did in the same era. Neither approach allows us to preserve both gospel-driven concern for this earth and anticipation of heaven.

To reconceive our lives in light of eternity only makes

sense. We will live on this earth, at the longest, for a hundred or so years. We will worship God in heaven for eternity. We all know that it is challenging to live for a realm that we cannot see, but really, is this not the paradox of our faith? We love a Savior we have not seen. Can we not live in anticipation of the heavenly realm where the Lord dwells and waits to receive His children?

Prioritizing Family

Sometimes we can act as if our family members will not live forever. That may sound strange to Christian readers, but practically, it applies to the way many families live on a day-to-day basis. We need to adopt and apply an eschatological mind-set for the sake of those we love. Our spouses, children, and extended family members will spend eternity in either heaven or hell. Remembering this simple reality will prod us out of complacence and cause us to approach all of our family interactions with care and a sense of gravity.

Instead of leaving witnessing to someone else, we can assume responsibility for this momentous task. We should not, for example, cede spiritual care of our children to another person, whether a youth minister, coach, or other authority figure, however gifted they may be. As parents, we need to shepherd our children and raise them in the fear and admonition of the Lord. We need to keep their lives in eternal perspective, carefully choosing what sins and attitudes to tackle at a given time. With unsaved extended family members, we should undertake, however awkward it may be, to share the gospel, realizing that their only hope for heaven is Jesus Christ. This is a key part of the eschatological mind-set. It is not the part we want to think much about, but we must do so if we are to honor God's Word.

We should adopt a way of life that will best enable us to care for our family members, particularly our children. Modern consumerism pushes us to sacrifice anything and everything for the sake of spending power and the accumulation of goods and experiences. Family is often sacrificed in the process. Christians who live with eternity in mind will find such a sacrifice impossible. In an individual sense, the most significant responsibility one can have is the care of a child. Every child has a soul; every soul is precious. Those parents who focus on this plain truth will find themselves fundamentally unable to yield primacy of focus and attention to anything but their children. This logic may seem strange to an unbeliever trying to get the most out of this world, but may make great sense to those who have different priorities and hopes for this life.

Christian parents will take up the work of parenting with concern that will seem strange to other families, who readily allow earthly priorities to shape the raising of children. Such leadership will not only serve the hearts and souls of children well, but will in the end function as a witness to a watching world of the significance of eternity. Children cannot be raised haphazardly, as if heaven and hell do not exist. The afterlife is real, and even in an age boasting far greater health care than

Edwards's, nothing is certain. Death can strike at any moment, and does. Christian parents must face this fact, allow it to guide their shepherding, and seize the opportunity to glorify the Lord and prepare their children to meet their Maker. Edwards, as we have seen, modeled this in his own family.

Loving Church

The modern era has dramatically reshaped the local church. In a climate flooded with self-help books and life-improvement tips, many churches have shaped themselves more as nurturers of the psyche than outposts of heaven storming the gates of hell. These assemblies oftentimes find receptive audiences, and many of them do preach the gospel and lead people to salvation in Christ. But their posture, their conception of church, leaves much to be desired.

Previous models of the local church have also suffered from notable weaknesses, as every model will. Some have presented the congregation as more of a communal rallying point, a place to celebrate shared heritage and common political views. Others have so identified with certain social causes that they have lost sight of the radical spirituality of the Bible. Some have construed the church merely as a place of moral formation, a safe zone for the training of children in certain behaviors and ideas. Others have viewed the church as something of a retreat center, a place to camp in their journey out of contact with the world and worldly people. We could list others, but the point is clear. Many local churches have, whether preaching the gospel or not, failed to embrace, teach, and embody an eschatological way of life.

Local churches have a great opportunity in this age. In a culture disconnected from traditional structures, many people today long for true community. As the church recovers its biblical identity as a group of Christians bonded by a common love for the Savior and growing in the knowledge and love of God, it can offer the lost around it a powerful picture of transformation and acceptance. Where many around us have no family, the people of God can become their family (Psalm 27:10).

The church today must remember that unlike every other institution and organization on this earth, it will transcend this world. All who truly know Christ will reign with Him in the new heavens and new earth (2 Timothy 2:12). While this earthly age endures, the church is thus a foretaste of heaven. It is to model an unearthly way of life, with standards of holiness that may seem quite strange to the lost. It enables its people to grow in the knowledge and love of God and floods the mind with truth that rouses the heart. It has a gospel to share, and is not simply a community improvement organization. It is concerned with doing good to all, but its mission is a spiritual one, and even the work of justice must point ultimately to the spiritual truths that undergird that work. Past generations have cared too little for good works in the public sphere, but it is also possible for churches to lose sight of their charter, of the body of doctrine that stamps them as otherworldly.

The church's eschatological nature requires that it not bend with every cultural wind, but storm through this world as a force for the Lord Jesus Christ. The church, however big or small it may be, is founded on the Word, loved by the Savior, and empowered by the Spirit. Its gospel is not small or weak. The preaching of the Word is not powerless or ineffective. The Bible is not tame or lifeless. The Christian faith is a force, a comet of righteousness moving through a universe darkened by sin. Many local churches practice a countercultural brand of Christianity that does not seek to tailor the message to the exact needs and wants of an unsaved audience, but rather presents the greatness of God and the glory of Christ in unapologetic terms. "Conversations" are out, and preaching is in. Younger Christians are flocking to high-cost Christianity and local-church life that calls for total commitment and offers an exalted view of God. Collin Hansen's insightful book *Young, Restless, and Reformed* chronicles this welcome development.

In whatever church context believers find themselves, they may act as agents of this brand of belief. The local church has primacy in the New Testament. It is founded by the Lord Jesus Christ, the only institution of this world so graced (Matthew 16:18). Eschatologically minded Christians will seek out biblically faithful churches and work in them for the glory of God and the good of all, just as Edwards did for all of his life. He threw himself into the work of the local church and never turned his back on it.

Edwards knew, as we must, that every believer and every gospel-preaching church is part of a kingdom movement, an offensive campaign planned by the Lord to take spiritual territory back from the adversary. The kingdom advances in large part through the work of the local church to promote and live out the gospel. This work of the kingdom sets the stage for the full realization of Christ's lordship over the earth in a day that will soon dawn (Matthew 24:14). Remembering one's place in this great movement and the value of every believer in the broader mission of the local church will lead believers to live self-sacrificing, counter-cultural, Christ-centered lives in these last days.

Invigorating Work

The eschatological mind-set also refigures our conception of work. All work, as Martin Luther so helpfully emphasized, is God's work. But our earthly vocations will one day end. We will serve the Lord in heaven, but all our career advances and vocational ambitions will soon lie beside us in the grave. We should esteem work, then, while keeping it in proper perspective, unlike so many in our society who fail on this point, and who destroy their souls in pursuit of economic dreams.

At the same time, we need to always remember that our earthly lives share a direct connection with our heavenly lives (1 Corinthians 10:31). The way we live here, as Edwards stressed in his preaching, directly affects our spiritual maturity and thus our heavenly standing (see Matthew 6:19; James 2). We must reject the anti-work spirit so common in our age, dramatized to great comedic effect in sitcoms and movies, and work with energy and intensity in our callings. All work done for the Lord is important. Every position, every vocation, allows us the opportunity to give God glory, whether we labor as a flower-shop owner, a stay-at-home mother, a bus driver, a corporate lawyer, or a writer. How we do the work given us in God's gracious providence matters greatly to Him (Colossians 3:23–24).

The dualism of times past, in which society accorded so-called "spiritual" work great esteem and devalued many other callings, has rightly faded into history. Nowadays, we know that all Christians possess countless opportunities to store up spiritual treasures in heaven. We need to apply this knowledge by approaching our crafts, callings, and vocations with the same intensity that Edwards did as a pastor. He worked tirelessly to give a good account for the hours given him for work. Similarly, we must see our daily vocations in eschatological terms. We should not work merely to accumulate possessions or finance expensive vacations. We have a greater motive for work than consumerism. The days are short, and work is often challenging, but if we can push through the sluggishness and malaise of this realm, we can store up treasure in a place where work and worship will come as easily as the air we breathe.

Renewing Minds

It is impossible to write about Jonathan Edwards and his kind of eternity-focused mindset without making reference to the development of the mind. Edwards knew that his mind was a gift from God, so he devoted great attention to cultivating and strengthening it. He wanted to serve God by thinking well with the time given him. Doing so would deepen all of his life and ministry and thereby bring God more glory—and Jonathan more eternal reward.

We should do the same today. In our discipleship to Christ, we should not grow lax upon conversion and cease to think hard about our faith. Our assent to the Lordship of Christ over all things should lead us to try to live life as fully and richly as possible. The way that we think affects the way that we live; the way that we live on this earth affects our status in eternity. Thus our minds are not disconnected from eternity but in fact have a deep impact on it. It was for this reason that the apostle Paul gave his call to the Roman Christians to "be transformed by the renewal of your mind" (Romans 12:2).

We can experience transformation by reading weighty theological works. In the writings of Augustine, Luther, Calvin, the Puritans, Edwards, and many others from history we will find much to chew on. We should not confine our reading only to Christian sources but should seek to better understand world and national history, philosophy, and politics. It will help us greatly to find a thoughtful Christian in our church and ask them to help us identify books that will enable us to think more deeply and thus live richer lives that bring God more glory. As we study the Scripture, learn theology, and train ourselves to critique and learn from secular thought, we will expand our understanding of God and His world, grow wiser in how we live and think, and experience the satisfaction of loving God with our mind (Matthew 22:37). In all of these things, we will honor the Lord's gift of mental ability and thus win glory for Him and eternal gain for ourselves.

Passionate Witness

How does an eschatologically minded Christian live amongst unbelievers? The eschatological mind-set relates directly to the privilege of Christian witness. As Christians, we cannot responsibly argue that evangelism falls only to the professionals. To be given the gospel is to be given the joyful task of passing it on. Some will prove more adept at this work than others, but every Christian not only gets to share the gospel, but take up an evangelistic—some would say "missional"—life modeled on the Great Commission of Matthew 28:16–20. This kind of life, which Christians have been practicing for centuries, stems from belief in the afterlife. Christians who do not evangelize have not, for one reason or another, looked closely enough at the content of their faith, which is rooted in eternity. The desire for unsaved people to escape the torments of hell and taste the joys of heaven is the central motivation of Christian witness (Romans 10).

If we have little drive to share the gospel and act as salt and light in our culture (Matthew 5:13–16), then we have not yet reckoned with eternity as we must. It is not enough that we ourselves are saved; we must work to rescue others as well. Like our Lord, the Ruler of every inch of heaven and earth, we need to allow our understanding of eternity to drive our behavior on earth. This will mean that we seek wherever we can to build relationships with lost people (as Jesus did—see Mark 2:13–17, for example), share the gospel with unbelievers (Romans 10), display holy character to show the effects of salvation (Matthew 5:16), and support Christians who are doing the same (see, for example, Luke 8:3 and 1 Corinthians 9:14). We should spend our money differently than lost people, use the hours given us differently than unbelievers, and conduct ourselves in ways distinct from those far off from the faith. This does not mean, however, that we disengage from the world. In fact, it means the opposite. Though we must proceed with caution, knowing that many believers have fallen away due to lack of care in their interaction with this world, we must be in our world in order to win it.

Too many of us act like the Pharisees who judged Jesus for spending time with unbelievers in seedy locations (Luke 15:2). Yet Jesus did so purely. We are not Christ, of course, and we should evaluate our limits accordingly. But with that said, we cannot claim that we are emulating our Lord or His apostles by staying away from the lost. As the Gospels and the book of Acts record, Jesus and His followers did the opposite. Recognizing the desperate condition of the sinner and the awesome power of the Spirit, they poured into the habitations and haunts of the lost, challenging Pharisees, speaking sober truths to drunkards, rebuking kings, admonishing prostitutes to seek the mercy of the Lord. As Jesus and the apostles went boldly into the territory of the enemy, so should we.

Doing so will require courage and faith. It is easy for Christians to retreat into their own subcultures. It is wonderful to love the body and to spend time with fellow church members and Christians. We are called to do so (Hebrews 10:25). But we can overdo it on this point, which is tempting in an age when many cultures are hostile to the gospel. If we are not intentional about getting involved in the lives of others, we can create a lifestyle that effectively walls us off from non-Christians—we meet for breakfast with Christian friends, call Christian friends on our lunch break, hang out with church members after the workday finishes, and go to the church gym —or other designated hangout place—at night. Again, many of these things are good, but when we only come into contact with Christians, we need to ask if we are not cordoning ourselves off from the world and hiding our light under a bushel (Matthew 5:14–16).

Though some of us witness more naturally than others, all of us should seek with great effort to reach out to the lost and win them to Christ. An eschatological mind-set prizes communion with the saints. It gives primacy to the church. But it also draws us to take the lost and their eternal plight seriously, and thus do what we can to befriend them and win them to Christ.

We will need much wisdom, accountability, and pastoral guidance on these matters. We cannot enter into a lifestyle of evangelism unthinkingly. But with considerable direction from our local church, we can successfully reorient our lives from "exclusionary" to "evangelistic." Furthermore, we can bless our

unsaved neighbors and friends in untold ways by sharing biblical wisdom and divine love with them. Non-Christians are
not simply targets for us, or numbers, but living, breathing
people who search for friendship, guidance, and happiness
just as we do. Our evangelism should include not only spiritual conversation, but all the fruits of a redeemed heart and
mind. We should not limit our witness to words only, but we
should serve and encourage in God's love and grace.

Though Edwards lived in a very different kind of society
than we do, he clearly practiced an evangelistic way of life.
He took up a difficult post on the colonial frontier late in life,
when many today retire, to try to win Native Americans,
among others, to saving faith in Jesus Christ. We might think
of the pastor as a starchy scholar, but his life tells a different
story, even as it calls us out of comfort and ease to a counter-
cultural, gospel-centered way of life.

Jonathan Edwards, Eschatological Christian

*W*e have sketched a vision of an eschatological life. There is much that we could add; our vision is regrettably brief. But we trust that the material of the previous chapters, coupled with the suggestions of this chapter, will provide much food for thought about how Christians may live in light of eternity. We have repeatedly stressed that we are dealing here not merely with some tweaks to an existing way of life, but with a radical, otherworldly existence that looks, feels, and sounds different from a worldly condition. In a remarkable way, Jonathan Edwards saw the significance and seriousness of eternity. His writings reveal a mind captivated by the afterlife and a heart gripped by the fragility of humanity.

In a way that most of us do not, Edwards looked long and hard at heaven and hell. He saw that each was real. He realized that he could not skate lightly over hell, tucking it into a doctrinal statement while never mentioning it or warning sinners about it. He *had* to preach about it, and to do so with textual faithfulness and biblically inspired imagination. Such preaching would not only warn the sinner, but drive him to the inexhaustible well of God's mercy. Hell had an evangelistic power, Edwards knew. The church and pastor who trifled with it, passed it over, or quickly moved over it did so to their own detriment and at the cost of full-bodied gospel witness.

On the other hand, heaven had definite character and shape, Edwards saw. It had a glory and depth that few preachers or theologians discovered and communicated. Even as faithful preaching on hell would inspire holy fear in the heart of the sinner, biblical preaching on heaven would set the heart soaring with hope. The great God who filled hell with terror simultaneously set love free to rush over the inhabitants of heaven. In passage after passage, Edwards sought to show his hearers just how marvelous heaven would be, though no words could do it justice. We see, then, that heaven and hell were meant to be preached together, each disclosing the importance of the other, each shedding light on our glorious God.

We need not write or speak like the pastor to honor his legacy and live as eschatological Christians. We do not need to be a pastor. We do not need to work in vocational ministry. We need only to grasp the realities that sit plainly before us and apply them to our lives, or rather, allow them to transform our hearts and minds such that we experience the joy and weight and significance of an eschatological life. We are born with eternity in our hearts, a wise man once declared, but our sin often blinds us to this fact (Ecclesiastes 3:11). We naturally drift to a world-focused mind-set, especially in a technological, consumerist, entertainment-obsessed world like our own. Here, everything that matters ultimately seems of little consequence, while everything of little consequence seems ultimately important. Sin, and Satan, and the very spirit of this death-cursed world urge us to live as we wish before oblivion overtakes and silences us. The Bible, however, tells a different story, a true one, which we cannot ignore. The after-life is real; heaven and hell exist; our souls will go to one or the other; the way we live and think in this life bears directly on the realm we end up in.

There is no time to waste on this earth. Every day presents us with the opportunity to advance the spiritual kingdom of our Lord and to contribute in ways great and small to the salvation of the lost and the strengthening of the found. We need more believers like Edwards—not pastors only, but Christians of all kinds who emulate the heroes of Hebrews 11 and live with another realm foremost on their mind.

Among his many writings, few texts demonstrate the Edwardsean eschatological mind-set, the kind we so desperately need, better than his letters to his children. Writing to his son Timothy, Edwards offered a model of the kind of purposeful, eternity-centered, large-God theology we need today:

THAT WHICH YOU MET WITH, in your passage from New York to Newark, which was the occasion of your fever, was indeed a remarkable mine, a dispensation full of instruction, and a very loud call of God to you, to make haste and not to delay in the great business of religion. If you now have that distemper, which you have been threatened with, you are separated from your earthly friends; none of them must come to see you; and if you should die of it, you have already taken a final and everlasting leave of them while you are yet alive, not to have the comfort of their presence and immediate care, and never to see them again in the land of the living. And if you have escaped that distemper, it is by a remarkable providence that you are preserved. And your having been so exposed to it, must certainly be a loud call of God, not to trust in earthly friends, or anything here below. Young persons are very apt to trust in parents and friends, when they are sick, or when they think of being on a deathbed. But this providence remarkably teaches you the need of a better friend, and a better parent, than earthly parents are; one who is everywhere present, and all-sufficient; that can't be kept off by infectious distempers; who is able to save from death or to make happy in death; to save from eternal misery and to bestow eternal life. (*Works* 16, 579)

Reminding his son of the Savior, the father concluded his letter:

THEREFORE, THERE IS your only hope; and in him must be your refuge, who invites you to come to him, and says, "He that cometh to me, I will in no wise cast out" [John 6:37]. Whatever your circumstances are, it is your duty not to despair, but to hope in infinite mercy through a Redeemer. For God makes it your duty to pray to him for mercy which would not be your duty, if it was allowable for you to despair. We are expressly commanded to call upon

God in the day of trouble; and when we are afflicted, then to pray. (*Works* 16, 580)

As we have said before, Edwards was no killjoy. He loved his children, and delighted in their company, but he also committed himself to the duty of preparing them for eternity. He did this with his offspring, with his wife, and with himself. After he fell ill from a vaccination gone wrong in 1758, the pastor, so ambitious and able, rapidly came near his death. The account of his passing by his doctor, William Shippen, shows that Jonathan took his own counsel seriously. He met his end with eternity fully in view, as Shippen related:

> AND NEVER DID ANY MORTAL man more fully and clearly evidence the sincerity of all his professions, by one continued, universal, calm, cheerful resignation, and patient submission to the divine will, through every stage of his disease, than he; not so much as one discontented expression, nor the least appearance of murmuring through the whole. And never did any person expire with more perfect freedom from pain;—not so much as one distorted hair—but in the most proper sense of the words, he really fell asleep. Death had certainly lost its sting, as to him. (Marsden, 494)

When a Christian lives with eternity in mind, shaping life in view of it, death truly does lose its sting. We see this in the example of Jonathan Edwards. Even as his vision dimmed to darkness, Edwards showed no fear. Through the blood of Christ, he had defeated his enemy and escaped the wrath of God. Through the power of the Spirit, he had lived a holy life and promoted the gospel of grace. As will one day be true of us if Christ tarries, he was going home; the struggles and pains of this earth over, the world of love just coming into sight.

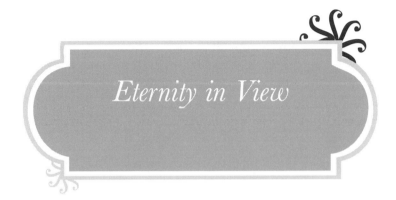

Eternity in View

*A*ll around us, people ignore the afterlife. They give their lives to chase fading things, things that glint with a cheap polish, catching our eye for an instant, offering satisfaction that lasts only as long. More than 250 years after his passing, Jonathan Edwards, America's greatest pastor-theologian, calls us to avoid this mortal mistake and seek a better realm. With all the heroes of Hebrews 11, and many more besides, Edwards's example cries out to us to leave this world and its hindrances behind. Through his sermons and writings, Edwards reaches across time to tell us of this place, this realm filled with delights that do not fade and happiness that will not end. A great cloud of witnesses joins him in this call. On the earth, "we have no lasting city," they cry over a great distance, so "seek the city that is to come" (Hebrews 13:14).

When we do, we will find that we are no longer alone. With all the faithful from all the ages and places of the earth, we will assemble as the bride of Christ. The Father has made us for this day, as Edwards explained in a sermon called "Approaching the End of God's Grand Design," based on Revelation 21:6. From before time, the Father desired:

> TO PRESENT TO HIS SON a spouse in perfect glory from amongst sinful, miserable mankind, blessing all that comply with his will in this matter and destroying all his enemies that oppose it, and so to communicate and glorify himself through Jesus Christ, God–man. (*Works* 25, 116)

Soon this day will come. Soon our days will close, and this world and its works will come to an end. Then the Son, resplendent in holiness, glorious in majesty, adorned in love, will approach the people of His possession, an alien and persecuted race, and take them as His bride, as Edwards outlined in his *History of the Work of Redemption*:

> AND WHEN CHRIST SHALL BRING his church into his Father's house in heaven after the judgment, he shall bring her there as his bride, having there presented her whom he loved and gave himself for to himself, without spot or wrinkle or any such thing. The bridegroom and the bride

shall then enter into heaven, both having on their wedding robes, attended with all the glorious angels. And there they enter on the feast and joys of their marriage before the Father; they shall then begin an everlasting wedding day. (*Works* 9, 508)

Amen. May that day come quickly.

Acknowledgments

We have a number of people to thank for the production of this volume.

We would like to thank Dave DeWit of Moody Publishers. Dave is an excellent editor and has been a tremendous help and encouragement in all aspects of the process. It was Dave who suggested that this project encompass not one book, but five, forming a comprehensive and definitive introductory series. We are thankful for his vision. We would also thank Chris Reese, who gave excellent feedback on this and every manuscript and made each book clearer and better.

We would like to thank Dr. John Piper for graciously providing a series foreword. It is a signal honor to have Dr. Piper involved in this project. Dr. Piper has enriched our understanding of Jonathan Edwards as he has for countless people. We are thankful to the Lord for his ministry, and we deeply appreciate his commendation of this collection. We greatly appreciate the assistance of David Mathis, Executive Pastoral Assistant to Dr. Piper.

We are deeply thankful for the love of our wives, Bethany Strachan and Wilma Sweeney. Without their support and sacrifice, this book could not have been written.

We would like to thank good friends who gave encouragement and counsel at various points in the project. Ralph and Faith Strachan, Ramzi and Susan Karam, Lester and Rachel Burgess, Drick and Cynthia Boyd, Melissa Green, and the entire Strachan family—thank you.

We dedicate this book to several Christians who have already left this earth. We remember Daniel Dustin, "Grandpa," a great man of God. For decades, he lived with heaven on his mind and taught his family to do the same. We remember the Revs. Paul Sweeney and Marvin Turner, men who labored in light of eternity and now taste their reward.

Above all others, we thank the King who purchased our redemption in His first coming. May He find His church faithful when He returns.

Recommended Resources on Jonathan Edwards

For the premier collection of Edwards's own writing, see *The Works of Jonathan Edwards*, vol. 1–26, Yale University Press. Access these works in their entirety free of charge at http://edwards.yale.edu.

For secondary sources, we recommend the following.

Introductory Reading

Byrd, James P. *Jonathan Edwards for Armchair Theologians.* Louisville, KY: Westminster John Knox Press, 2008.

McDermott, Gerald R. *Seeing God: Jonathan Edwards and Spiritual Discernment.* Vancouver: Regent College Publishing, 2000.

Nichols, Stephen A. *Jonathan Edwards: A Guided Tour of His Life and Thought*. Phillipsburg, NJ: Presbyterian & Reformed, 2001.

Storms, Sam. *Signs of the Spirit: An Interpretation of Jonathan Edwards' Religious Affections*. Wheaton, IL: Crossway Books, 2007.

Deeper Reading

Gura, Philip F. *Jonathan Edwards: America's Evangelical*. New York: Hill & Wang, 2005.

Kimnach, Wilson H., Kenneth P. Minkema, and Douglas A. Sweeney, eds. *The Sermons of Jonathan Edwards: A Reader*. New Haven: Yale University Press, 1999.

Lesser, M. X. *Reading Jonathan Edwards: An Annotated Bibliography in Three Parts, 1729–2005*. Grand Rapids: Eerdmans, 2008

Marsden, George. *Jonathan Edwards: A Life*. New Haven: Yale University Press, 2003.

McDermott, Gerald R., ed. *Understanding Jonathan Edwards: An Introduction to America's Theologian*. New York: Oxford University Press, 2009.

Moody, Josh. *The God-Centered Life: Insights from Jonathan Edwards for Today*. Vancouver: Regent College Publishing, 2007.

Murray, Iain H. *Jonathan Edwards: A New Biography.* Edinburgh: Banner of Truth Trust, 1987.

Piper, John. *God's Passion for His Glory: Living the Vision of Jonathan Edwards.* Wheaton, IL: Crossway Books, 1998.

————, and Justin Taylor, eds. *A God Entranced Vision of All Things: The Legacy of Jonathan Edwards.* Wheaton, IL: Crossway Books, 2004.

Smith, John E., Harry S. Stout, and Kenneth P. Minkema, eds. *A Jonathan Edwards Reader.* New Haven: Yale University Press, 1995.

Sweeney, Douglas A. *Jonathan Edwards and the Ministry of the Word: A Model of Faith and Thought.* Downers Grove, IL: InterVarsity Press, 2009.

BRINGING YOU THE TIMELESS CLASSICS

Classics

Selected for their enduring influence and timeless perspective …

Answers to Prayer
ISBN-13: 978-0-8024-5650-2

The Confessions
of St. Augustine
ISBN-13: 978-0-8024-5651-9

How to Pray
ISBN-13: 978-0-8024-5652-6

The Imitation of Christ
ISBN-13: 978-0-8024-5653-3

The Pilgrim's Progress
ISBN-13: 978-0-8024-5654-0

The True Vine
ISBN-13: 978-0-8024-5655-7

Power Through Prayer
ISBN-13: 978-0-8024-5662-5

The Christian's Secret
of a Happy Life
ISBN-13: 978-0-8024-5656-4

Hudson Taylor's
Spiritual Secret
ISBN-13: 978-0-8024-5658-8

MOODY
PUBLISHERS
MoodyClassics.com

BRINGING YOU THE TIMELESS CLASSICS
Classics

... these are key books that every believer on the journey of spiritual formation should read.

Holiness
ISBN-13: 978-0-8024-5455-3

Born Crucified
ISBN-13: 978-0-8024-5456-0

Names of God
ISBN-13: 978-0-8024-5856-8

The Overcoming Life
ISBN-13: 978-0-8024-5451-5

All of Grace
ISBN-13: 978-0-8024-5452-2

The Secret
of Guidance
ISBN-13: 978-0-8024-5454-6

The Incomparable Christ
ISBN-13: 978-0-8024-5660-1

Orthodoxy
ISBN-13: 978-0-8024-5657-1

The Apostolic Fathers
ISBN-13: 978-0-8024-5659-5